M000170326

SECRETS AND RIVALS

SECRETS AND RIVALS

Wartime Letters and the Parents I Never Knew

R. Bruce Larson

LIBRARY OF
· CONGRESS
SURPLUS
DUPLICATE

University of Missouri Press
Columbia

Copyright © 2015 by
The Curators of the University of Missouri
University of Missouri Press, Columbia, Missouri 65201
Printed and bound in the United States of America
All rights reserved. First printing, 2015.

ISBN: 978-0-8262-2052-3
Library of Congress Control Number: 2015940590

This paper meets the requirements of the
American National Standard for Permanence of Paper
for Printed Library Materials, Z39.48, 1984.

Page design and composition: BooksByBruce.com
Typefaces: Weiss, Ristretto

Dedication

To my parents

Epigraph

How they live on, those giants of our childhood, and how well they manage to take even death in their stride because although death can put an end to them right enough, it can never put an end to our relationship with them. Wherever or however else they may have come to life since, it is beyond a doubt that they live still in us.

—Frederick Buechner, *The Sacred Journey*

Contents

Author's Note / ix

1. At the End, in the Beginning / 1

2. Then, Now / 9

Acknowledgments / 189

Questions for Discussion / 191

Notes / 193

Author's Note

This book is nonfiction. Most details appear as they do in the originals, except that I changed some names and personal details to safeguard people's privacy. All quotations are verbatim; in a few instances, for readability, I shifted sentence or word order, altered punctuation slightly, or inserted words, which are denoted by brackets. Quotations with ungrammatical constructions or misspelled or underlined words appear that way in the letters. Italicized passages are not factual but represent my imagination or recollection of actual events.

The nearly seven hundred letters in Ruth's collection fill ten 2-inch ringed binders; some are quite long, and most discuss many topics. Almost all were written during World War II, but they mention only several sites of the war—the *Reuben James*, Guadalcanal, Truk, Kiska. Military censorship cannot account for this dearth of war news, since only about two dozen letters were subject to it. Instead, I believe, the paucity of war news reflects the writers' desire to conduct their lives as normally as possible; omitting war news helped to do that. I've tried to maintain this approach, inserting historical information only when necessary for clarification.

A good part of my professional work has involved the construction and interpretation of texts. When I was working as a cultural anthropologist I collected information from interviews with people and tried to create accounts that, along with my observations and experiences, mirrored the reality conveyed by the people with whom I spoke. Here I used the letters in a similar way. I compensated for the differences in time frame (the letters were written many decades ago) and the dearth of supporting information (because the writers were dead, I could not interview them) by juxtaposing my reconstruction and family lore. My memories of experiences with my parents provided another important source of information.

My professional background could take me only so far. After all, I wasn't writing an abstract treatise; I was writing about my parents. I couldn't, and never tried to, be objective. Even so, time provided the distance I needed to perceive them in their broader humanity beyond their parental roles. Reaching across the decades also allowed me to enter another world, a world when my parents were trying to find themselves. This world of difference invited me to experience my parents as I'd never experienced them before and to write a story I'd never known. Doing so has helped me to better understand myself. Indeed, even without the opportunity to explore a treasure trove left by a parent, we all can reflect on family stories and how family lore shaped our understanding of our parents and of ourselves. I found that the more I learned, the more I realized that the story needed to be shared.

R. B. L.

SECRETS AND RIVALS

1

At the End, in the Beginning

Our mother, Ruth, lay in her bed at the nursing home. "Evergreen," its name promised, but the sap of her life was fast running out. Shriveled and small, she labored for breath. The room was dark and cluttered with the detritus of her eighty-eight years—an old Swedish hymnal, a well-worn Bible, faded photographs, closets jam-packed with clothes.

My sister, brother, and I had gathered for the last good-byes. In addition to telling family stories, singing the old hymns, and praying together, we had the joyless task of sorting through her things—clothes, the motorized lounger, the bedroom set. And, in a closet, a box of letters that until then we hadn't known existed. These letters had followed her from World War II through her life—Minnesota, Wisconsin, California, Chicago and its suburbs, the ranch in Montana, the cabin in Michigan, and now to Evergreen.

Ruth saved things. She had come of age during the Great Depression, when scarcity had urged frugality. In addition, the objects she saved helped her to remember meaningful events—"the birth of our first grandchild" or "when we tipped over on that canoe trip"—and, even more, it served to help her relive past emotions. Near the end, next to her lounger she kept shopping bags filled with old cards and letters. The date didn't matter nor, as the years went by, did the content. What mattered was the warmth she felt surrounded by expressions of love.

Ruth's hoarding required space. Luckily she had access to plenty of it. During the years when we three children were still at home, she had "the little back bedroom," which took on the role of miniwarehouse for Ruth's burgeoning collection of clippings, cards, and letters. These she put into boxes or just stacked in piles against the walls and in the corners.

As the little back bedroom filled, other space became available. The family built a lakeside cottage in Upper Michigan complete with basement, second story, and lots of attic room. Ruth's accumulations overflowed into chests, boxes, and drawers—even the sauna. In her declining years she became repetitive, saying often: "My, but you'll have a lot of papers to go through when I'm gone."

The most significant of those papers was a box of nearly seven hundred letters from World War II. Ruth had saved the letters through move after move, down to that last room in the nursing home, so that they were one of the few things she clung to at the end. Her feelings about those letters amounted to a yearning—powerful enough to persist through sixty-five years—that someone pay attention to those letters. They couldn't be discarded unread.

My siblings suggested that my wife, Katherine, and I take the letters to the family cottage, where we were staying during this farewell weekend in 2009. We arrived there cold and tired but not yet ready to sleep, so we settled in by the fire, intending to organize the letters chronologically. With almost all still in their original envelopes, the task looked like just the mindless project we needed to help us unwind.

After a few minutes I stopped. We had thought that these were all love letters from my father, but I had come upon a letter from a man I'd never heard of. A moment later Katherine found a postcard from a different man. How did those other guys get in there? As we looked further through the letters, we found still more from various men. Curious, I slid one out of its envelope, unfolded it, and began to read.

I hadn't expected to read more than a handful because I believed the letters would contain little more than sentimentalities. Love letters, even if penned by one's parents, don't often reveal new things. Everyday language is typically inadequate to bring freshness to universal experiences. But after just a few letters I was hooked. Not only did they open to me a period of family history about which I had known little, they also showed me aspects of my parents' characters that I'd never encountered.

And I was stunned. I had thought I knew my parents; after all, we had lived in the same household for eighteen years and kept in regular contact for decades. The letters, however, showed me that I didn't—at least not in the way I thought I did. They reflected a world very different from the one I had expected to find. Ruth's collection proved confusing, disorienting, life changing—ultimately, a profound gift.

Before I wrote the story, I organized the letters in notebooks and transcribed them to the computer. I obtained the military service records of my father, Bob; microfilm of period newspapers; and Ruth's university transcript. I contacted federal and state courts in Minnesota and Wisconsin. I visited places where some of these events transpired.

The account that emerged challenged my previous assumptions about my parents and expanded what I knew about them in ways I could scarcely imagine. It's their story, but it's my version of their story, the version I needed to write in order to make sense of what

I had learned from the letters. My two siblings experienced our parents, our family interactions, and family lore differently, and their versions of these stories would differ too.

•

What Adam Kirsch wrote in a different historical context applies as well to the function of family lore: "The present is always lived in ambiguity. It is only in retrospect that we begin to simplify experience into myth—because we need stories to live by, because we want to honor our ancestors and our country instead of doubting them." But the process of mythologizing exacts a price: "In this way, a necessary but terrible war is simplified into a 'good war,' and we start to feel shy or guilty at any reminder of the moral compromises and outright betrayals that are inseparable from every combat."[1]

Just as postwar retrospectives "simplify experience into myth" for nations, so lore functions for families. Typically family lore ignores especially stressful experiences or morally repugnant actions so that the stories end up showing family members in a positive light. If a negative story survives as an element of family lore—"when Dad lost his job" or "when Mom almost died"—it's included to exemplify gumption, triumph over hard times, fortitude in the face of near-disaster, often in the comfortable certitude of hindsight. As family lore develops, it contributes to family identity, providing stories to guide, and tales to inspire, future generations.

Lore functioned a little differently in my family, especially when it was about my father. He resisted saying much about his childhood years because he didn't want "to give you kids any ideas." From the little I did hear, he had good reason to exercise restraint. He was a hellion, and we were told the tales as examples of behavior to avoid. Thus there was the Sunday afternoon when he told his parents that he was leaving for a youth meeting at church. What he didn't say was that he had just tossed his ice skates out his bedroom window and was heading to the rink instead. Several hours later the doorbell rang; there he was, face bloodied, in the custody of a police officer.

Another story was about my dad and his buddies' jumping onto the back of a streetcar as it pulled away from a stop; they hoped to hang on without detection long enough to make it to the next stop. In yet another story they dared each other to drive fast onto a bridge and slam on the brakes while jerking the steering wheel so that the car skidded. The one whose car stopped closest to the edge won.

As for the father I knew during my earliest years, my experience was mixed. I remember stumbling as a toddler because my pants rode too low. Dad teased me, saying, "What's the matter, Broop, can't keep your pants up?" I began to cry, but he just called me "Droopy Drawers." Maybe he wanted to show affection, but I felt humiliated. Later in life I noticed that he relished seeing people struggle, often pointing them out to me while chuckling at their plight. This struck me as odd, and I wondered how he could be so insensitive. In emergencies, though, he showed tenderness. I remember the first time the big kids let me climb into the tree house. When it was time to leave, I looked down and then burst into tears. My brother ran for Dad and he rescued me. Another time I crashed my bike into a mailbox and bloodied my nose. Again he offered comfort.

Mostly, though, my father conveyed emotional neutrality. A well-cut lawn might elicit a word or two of recognition, but little else did. Perhaps he feared the outcome of too much praise—I remember when he chastised my mother for complimenting me on my solo after a band concert; he said her comment might go to my head. I don't remember him reaching out to me with a hug.

As I grew into adulthood, I blamed my father for not giving me the emotional support I craved. Writing this book has helped me to understand why he could not.

Family lore about my mother focused on her role as the daughter of a small-town Baptist pastor. From birth she had been pinned under the microscope of her father's watchful congregants as well as that of a father whose utterances rivaled those of the ancient Hebrew prophets. She was also the youngest of five children and the only girl.

In the first part of the twentieth century, these Swedish American Baptists advocated a life of piety marked by daily Bible reading and prayer, regular church attendance—once on Wednesdays, twice on Sundays—and a long list of thou-shalt-nots: profanity, alcohol, dances, movies, card games, gambling, and sex outside marriage. The preacher's family would be expected to live this way, especially by members of small-town congregations like those served by Ruth's father. Any deviation would be noticed and reprobated. According to family lore, my mother was a model preacher's kid.

Ruth's high school years in Balsam Lake, Wisconsin—years that she spoke of with fondness but little detail—were crowned by her graduation as valedictorian of her small class, which she referred to as "the class of eight in '38." Family lore therefore pegged her as a fine student, confirmed by a nursing degree from the University of Minnesota and her work as a registered nurse.

My earliest experiences of my mother revolved around her provision of basic care—cooking meals, washing clothes, and so on. When I was very young, she sometimes sang lullabies at bedtime. Later she drove me to music lessons and church youth group meetings. I remember my mother's remarking how she enjoyed our occasional late-evening talks around the kitchen table during my adolescent years. Unlike my father, she complimented me for grades and other accomplishments. Though she rarely spoke of her love, she hugged me often and I felt loved.

In fact, ever since I can remember, my mother called me her "perfect baby." As I grew older, she continued the charade, if only in jest, to my great discomfort. I was always confused about her motive. Writing this book has helped me to understand it.

Family lore, as I heard it, was dead silent about any romance in my parents' prewedding lives. But the letters to Ruth from men other than my father challenged that silence. What else, I wondered, had my mother not told me? And what about Bob? What might the letters tell me about him that I never knew? And what else happened to them during these years that had lasting impact on them and so indirectly on me?

Then, broader questions: How well can children know their parents? Do the role definitions of family structure—parents always parents, children always children—prevent parents from sharing more completely about their past? Is it better for children if parents refrain from telling stories describing their vulnerability, or should parents share more openly their less-than-exemplary history?

So I delved into Ruth's letters. For a while I found it hard to accept what I wasn't prepared to learn. As I spent more and more time with the letters, though, reflection gave way to insight. I began to see my parents quite differently. As the letters delivered surprise after surprise, I had to revisit everything I had thought I knew and then to revise, expand, or overturn my understanding of family lore.

2

Then, Now

Since I'd never known Bob and Ruth before they were my parents and on the verge of middle age, I had difficulty at first imagining them as young and single, and I had no idea how they met. Perhaps I had internalized the fairy tale ideal that, whatever happened before the wedding, their marriage was all that mattered. To be sure, courtship can yield its quirky stories, but their marriage made the difference. Everything leading up to that was chaff that I, unaffected, could blow away. Or so I assumed.

Their beginning was as mundane as a hot Sunday afternoon in July 1941. While Ruth and her roommate, Veronica Olson, enjoyed an outing at Medicine Lake near Minneapolis, they struck up a conversation with two young men, Bob, and his cousin Arvid. Ruth must have impressed Bob, because the next morning he used his employer's stationery to write:

Dear Ruthie:
How's the kid? I'll bet you're kind of surprised to hear from Rochester—How'd the show at Lake Calhoun turn out? Hope it was pretty good. Say, Kiddo—when you aren't too busy I'd appreciate hearing from you—(course I know how terribly busy

nurses are—) Was wondering if you had every Sunday off or how your arrangement was—Yours

Bob

Twenty-year-old Ruth responded right away with an enthusiastic four-page gush:

Dear Bob:

Was I ever surprised to get your letter! When Veronica was talking to her mother on the phone Tuesday afternoon, her mother said to tell me that I had a letter there from Rochester. I couldn't figure out who it was from and just about died of curiosity until I got it that night. You really put one over on me 'cuz I never dreamed of hearing from you. How did you ever remember Veronica's address?

The water parade at Lake Calhoun was beautiful. Then we happened to stand right near where the fireworks were shot off so we didn't know if we were all in one piece or not when we got home. Too bad you missed it but I s'pose you had to go back to Rochester.

Yes, nurses are such busy people but it seems to me that everyone is always busy nowadays or doesn't life affect you that way?

No, I very seldom have Sunday off—last Sunday was one of those rare ones but we usually have some time off.

Do you come home every week-end or don't you have every Sunday off either? If you'll be home this Sunday why don't you stop in and I'll show you the pictures we took at Medicine Lake last Sunday—they're good—at least the one you took is swell. I'm sure I'll be here until church time.

Yours,

Ruthie

Scuse the scribblin' but I gotta go on duty. The Nurses Home is on 6th Avenue & 6th St.

'Bye now!

Then, Now

When I first read that exchange, I chuckled. Bob and Ruth were young enough then to be my children now. I was born in 1953 and never lived through a time like the early 1940s, nor did I hear much about what that time was like for them. Then I realized that my experiences in college teaching and campus ministry could help me understand where my parents were developmentally at this point in their lives. Filtering the letters through the lens of my professional work with young adults helped me to interpret what I read. Still, I spent months with what I found in the letters before I began to feel comfortable seeing my parents as young adults.

I knew, of course, that Bob, the only child of Swedish immigrants, had grown up in Minneapolis and that he had landed his first job at the Otis Elevator Company in Rochester seventy-five miles away, where he then lived. Ruth's letters filled in some details. He started in the office and then switched to working in the field as a mechanic's helper. He hadn't a car, so, when he couldn't borrow Arvid's, he hopped a bus to travel between the two cities. Living in Rochester while Ruth was in Minneapolis presented a challenge, but he knew what to do. He would write.

This was an era of letter writing. Not everyone had access to a telephone, and in many communal living situations—military barracks, for example, or the Nurses Home, where Ruth and Veronica lived—one telephone served many. People used telephones primarily for communicating brief messages such as making an appointment, not for extended conversations. For urgent messages they sent telegrams; for the rest, letters.

As with social media today, letter writing of that era provided much more than a substitute for communicating in person. Correspondents could conduct extended conversations and express feelings that they may not have been comfortable voicing in person. But there were profound limitations to relationships built mostly on letters. Expressing feelings is one thing; discussing them is quite another. Presenting a partial image on paper is one thing;

experiencing the reality of a person is quite another. Planning the next date on paper is one thing; adapting to the vagaries of real life is quite another. Letters alone cannot overcome such limitations.

The logistics of letter writing in the 1940s also contributed to the stunting of relationships that depended on exchanging letters. Getting a response took time, during which the emotional and mental state of the writer usually had shifted. To fully understand the response required that the writer remember not only what she had written but her underlying feelings and thoughts as well. Since daily letters were common during these years, it was impossible to keep track of how one had felt and thought while writing each one. Every letter arrived as a tangle of many strands.

"Say, Drop Me a Line"

The collection contained letters Ruth received before that first letter from Bob. I found others from Fred (1939), Will (1940), and Len (1939–40); Len's letters shed light on how Ruth had entered nurses' training. In 1939 she attended a small Swedish Baptist school, Bethel College in St. Paul. Len, a musician at the Children's Gospel Mission in Minneapolis, urged her to put her musical talents to work in his missionary ministry.

According to family lore, Ruth had wanted to be a doctor. When she told her father, he advised her to become a nurse because "only men are doctors." Since Bethel didn't offer a nursing program, she enrolled in River Falls Teachers College to take care of some prerequisites and then, in 1940, transferred to the reputable nursing program at the University of Minnesota.

With her small-town conservative background, Ruth's experience of a large school in a big city brought culture shock. Len worried about the university "where sin abounds on every hand," but hoped that she would "still come out untainted and unstained from your worldly environment." He concluded: "It'll be good for you Ruth, make you strong in the Lord and help you to rely on him and keep you on your knees a lot."

Beyond the cultural challenges, nursing school brought imposing demands. Graduates later reminisced about working split shifts of eight hours daily between 7 A.M. and 7 P.M. with classes in between and only one day off each week. They studied during the rest of their waking hours and reported limiting their occasional socializing to a swim in Lake Calhoun or a movie in downtown Minneapolis. In the mid-1940s about a third of each entering class quit in the first year. As one retired nurse recalled her student days, "We learned right away if nursing was right for us." Another noted that the program was "intense, unforgettable, and life-changing."[1] Successful completion required commitment and stamina.

As a transfer student Ruth avoided that brutal first year of nursing school. By the time she met Bob in the summer of 1941, she'd weathered her sophomore year and had two more to go before graduation.

Bob saw Ruth again in Minneapolis on August 3 and wrote afterward, summoning the courage to add this postscript: "Thanks for the swell time you gave me yesterday—First time I've felt that good for a heck of a long time." In her first letter Ruth had tucked an important intimacy—her address—into her postscript. Now Bob, too, saved intimacy for his PS. They were enjoying each other.

"I Certainly Feel Swell
When I Remember <u>That</u> Night"

Their next outing at Berger Lake had lasting impact. Bob reminisced months later that he "often thought of Berger's Lake and that Sunday afternoon," even though "we really didn't do any swimming at all." He was able to put "a lot of things straight in my mind as to what was what." In another letter he again recalled "Berger's Lake where you had your black swim suit on—whew, honey—you do things to me."

If that swim date launched the relationship, the next one at Lake of the Isles put it into orbit. It happened on a rainy September Sunday, but the rain did nothing to detract from the magic. Bob reminisced months later about "our evening by Lake of the Isles with the blanket and radio and drifting canoes interrupting us." Another time, when he felt miserable after two nights of rain, he heard "September in the Rain" on the radio and recalled "how swell the rain was so that I don't feel gloomy any more. Especially when I remember <u>that</u> night." Indeed the date held such power that he blurted in a December letter how much he wanted this new relationship to be more than a summer fling: "I really meant what I said when I asked you if you'd marry me sometime. Honey, when I asked you that I was never more serious in my life."

At this point I started wondering whether I should be entering into these private moments in my parents' lives. Ruth had carefully protected her letters for decades—why didn't she explicitly tell me or my siblings that they existed? The letters recall personal experiences during a historic epoch, but they also include experiences of deep pain and, later, profound guilt. Why would she want to remember those? Perhaps she began just from a habit of saving. Or perhaps she saved them to remember the years when so many men gave her so much attention. As the years passed, sentiment might have clouded her memory until she wasn't able to recall all of what the letters contained. So she saw them as a connection to a time long gone or as a personification of lessons learned or as a record of her life's fulcrum.

Whatever rationale led her to save the letters, did her silence mean she intended their secrets to be kept? If she ever contemplated sharing them while she was alive, shame—that effective silencer—would have stopped her cold. I believe that, unable to tell anyone of those secrets while she was alive, she hoped that the letters would do the job after she died. This explains why she saved the letters without telling her children and why she didn't destroy them long ago. It also matches her tendency to deal with sensitive situations passively. Thus in her final years she referred simply to "the many papers" that her middle-aged children would have "to go through after I'm gone." Another strand of evidence confirms to me that Ruth wanted the content of the letters known. When she at last moved into the nursing home, space limitations demanded that she bring only her most precious things. She chose these letters. Perhaps she intended to go through them herself, or perhaps she hoped that keeping them near would make finding them easier after she died. We did find them easily.

Back in 1941 those idyllic dates by Minnesota lakes took place against the rumblings of war—war that had already engulfed Europe and parts of Asia and was soon to sweep globally. The U.S. military draft had begun the previous fall, and many young men were enlisting. Some were motivated by patriotism or a feeling that fascism needed to be stopped. Others acted out of sheer pragmatism. Enlisting gave them a chance of entering the branch of military service that they wanted. Better to enlist and have a choice, they figured, than to wait, be drafted, and have no choice.

Bob's letters give no hint of patriotism or fear of fascism, but he was indeed pragmatic. On October 8 he enlisted in the U.S. Coast Guard and was sent to Port Townsend, forty miles northwest of Seattle at the headwaters of Puget Sound. After a week of training

Bob began his first letter as a Coastie to Ruth: "Don't know how to start but here's telling you rite off the bat that I'm so lonesome I don't know what to do." With "guys sleeping on the floor" in "pretty crowded" conditions, he was "standing up riting," and he apologized for "the scribbling" and asked that "you drop me a few letters."

Bob would be trained in such areas as semaphore signals, splicing ropes, tying knots, martial arts, marching, and riflery. His efforts soon brought him recognition as a member of the senior color guard. "Guys are sure giving me the razz," he noted, "but I can't help it cuz Commander picked me."

This would have been heady stuff for Bob. I knew that his high school career had been unimpressive; Central High in Minneapolis had discharged him before graduation. If Minnehaha Academy, a private Christian school, hadn't taken him in, he probably wouldn't have received a diploma. Whatever other challenges military service would present, for the first time he was beginning to experience success and, even more unusual, recognition.

Pleased as he was, a battalion review prompted fretting: "This will either make me or break me as far as my relation with the Company Commander." And an even greater unknown loomed as "all the officers take the attitude we are now at war—Makes a guy feel funny inside."

When I first read that, I was struck by my father's expression of feeling. He wasn't one to express vulnerability, at least not around me. Now I see that his use of *a guy* instead of *me* reflected his awkwardness, a linguistic way to distance himself from that feeling.

Bob continued to express feelings. His next letter spoke of being so down from "the blues" that he "would almost contemplate desertion if the consequences weren't so great." And he was "getting hard up for some good necking" and even hoped to "be home (IN BED) with you."

My eyes widened, not because I was surprised that my father wrote that—as noted, according to family lore, he was a hellion— but I didn't imagine that he would have been so aggressive, and so soon, in the relationship. Somehow I had picked up the erroneous notion that premarital sex didn't become common until the sexual revolution in the 1960s. My father was teaching me in ways he could never have anticipated.

I also assumed, mistakenly again, that my mother would immediately put a stop to such advances. After all, Len had urged her to stay "untainted and unstained" from the sin abounding "on every hand." Because I knew of her strong faith in my time, I expected her to follow that advice then. But she didn't have to, at least here, because Bob pulled back: "I don't want to do anything where the feeling wasn't mutual." Later he clarified: "I hope you get what I mean and don't think some of it's too rough (about the hard up part I mean)."

Bob retreated from his sexually explicit banter, but his loneliness dragged on. At one point he suggested, "Maybe we better not talk about lonesomeness." Another time, when "most of the boys went out to a football game," he didn't feel like going anywhere. Instead he "looked over the snapshots" taken the day he left Minneapolis. But all he could articulate was a "funny feeling." Two days later, after not having heard from Ruth "for about 4 days now," Bob speculated, "Maybe that's why I'm so blue." In his next letter he lashed out: "Hope you're plenty lonesome—then you'll know how I feel—course you're lucky—you got all your old friends and I've got to make 'em."

Bob's growing dependence on Ruth's letters put him at emotional risk. If he didn't receive a letter within a day or two, especially when he was "feeling blue," he descended into anxious waiting while fretting that another man might be wooing her. When gaps between her letters were longer—to him a few days seemed like a month—he began to doubt whether she was remaining true. When there were "still no letters," he worried more: "What's the matter, honey, did I say something wrong."

Each letter relieved Bob and eased his anxiety. He would immediately start waiting for the next one, but he found the wait unnerving. If gaps grew especially long, "to be exact six days," he goaded: "Come on kid, let's hear how things are—How many guys you've gone out with and all that 'stuff.'" When, in yet another letter, he speculated that perhaps "Sammy's in town," he fidgeted that "you've got me worried."

Soon Bob found himself unable to relax and enjoy the thought of "my little honey: Every time I think of that phrase I start thinking of your classes at the U and how long you'll be my honey." He hoped that she would "be sure and remember me when it comes to all those parties" and that she wouldn't "get too busy over the coming holidays and forget your little swede boy friend." In his confident moments he could joke: "I thought you were going to study when I was gone."

Bob's expressions of depression, loneliness, worry, and emotional dependency showed a side of him that I had never seen. The father I observed depended on my mother for his physical needs, but I don't recall ever hearing him express feelings like sadness or worry. Perhaps he feared getting into an argument, a violation of their policy not to argue in front of the children. Or maybe his outlook had changed by the time I knew him. Whatever the case, the unspoken message I picked up was that feelings, if they existed, were to be repressed.

The start of my own first marriage, to Suzie in my early twenties, showed how well I had internalized that message. I had great difficulty even identifying my feelings, much less expressing them. Getting into an argument utterly disoriented me; I shut down, numb and silent. Understandably this frustrated Suzie and the argument would escalate. Later, when she described growing up in a "conflict-oriented family," I realized that I had never witnessed a spousal spat. I had no model to show me how to fight. In order to grow in marriage, I had to learn how to identify my feelings and share them. With hard work over several years I gained confidence in doing this, and we began to address our disagreements more productively.

Discovering this new dimension of my father's emotionality ushered me into uncharted territory in middle age. Sometimes his feelings burst so forcefully from the page that they moved me to tears. I knew that emotions have no expiration date, but I felt confounded by the raw immediacy of his pain crying out to me across seven decades. The Christian belief in "the communion of the saints"—that living people connect spiritually with those who are dead—came to mind, but this proved insufficient to address my confusion. Then I thought of societies that use rituals, dreams, spiritual visitations, and the like to communicate with ancestors, but that was scarcely part of my emotional tool box. All I could do, I concluded, was appreciate my father's feelings as they leaped to life again as I read from yellowed pages.

Why had I never experienced him like this? Where had that part of him gone? Was I somehow responsible? I felt that the guy who was writing these letters was someone other than my father.

It was becoming increasingly clear that I needed to take a critical look at family lore. As in most families, lore had supplied me with answers to my childhood questions about my family and its background. I'd never had a reason to reflect on what I had so uncritically absorbed, and it lay dormant for decades. Now, upon retrieval, I realized that lore didn't prepare me to find my father expressing any feelings, much less a range of them. This dimension of his character, so stunningly new to me, demanded that I revise my understanding.

"If at Any Time You Need Money"

In addition to Bob's growing emotional dependency on Ruth, another bond was building between them. In his first letter from Port Townsend, Bob enclosed twenty dollars—more than a week's pay—and instructed Ruth to keep fifteen dollars for her own use and give the rest to his parents. He had known her for less than three months, so I was surprised to see him handing over his money to her so soon. She proposed a joint account. A joint account? I was dubious. But he consented, so long as "you're able to get the money out without any red tape."

Perhaps Bob felt forced to consent because "nothing's safe around here and I might be transferred overnight." Or perhaps he was enacting a strategy. Having her manage his funds, he may have hoped, would bind Ruth closer to him. At the same time she might appreciate him more because he gave her free access to his funds.

Ruth continued to play banker for Bob. He sent her his paychecks; she sent him spending money. Though he expressed concern about how much he could get "in case I wire you quick as in an emergency," he seemed content with the arrangement. With each request Ruth came through: "Thanks darling. I can really depend on you," he replied.

Bob initiated a parallel effort to involve Ruth with his family back home. He suggested, asked, and sometimes demanded that she make phone calls or personal visits to his parents and other relatives: "Hope you're taking advantage of my relations hospitality, If not, why not? Don't forget, honey, you've got to keep the diplomacy up for both of us while I'm gone."

Bob's hopes for successful diplomacy hinged on Ruth's connecting frequently with his mother, a key figure in his life. A hen with one chick, she had fretted when she learned of his plan to enlist. His choice of the U.S. Coast Guard—generally assumed to offer the best chance of avoiding combat—would have brought only temporary relief. No wonder, then, that Bob often directed Ruth to calm his mother, to "tell her the good news" or to let her "know that I'm O.K."

Bob mentioned his father only to report reactions to Ruth, noting how his father was "extremely pleased" with her, that "he sure raves about you" and "thinks the world of you." His father may have felt pleased with Ruth, but her father hardly felt the same way about Bob: "I'm afraid your Dad's going to have to change his mind about me—But we'll see later," Bob wrote Ruth. After two weeks "later" arrived: "Was kind of surprised. Thought you were kidding when you said he'd write."

In the Swedish American community in which Bob had grown up, extended family was as important as immediate family. This was especially true for Bob, an only child, who treated his cousins like siblings. Ruth already knew Cousin Arvid, and she had met Bob's parents. Bob now took steps to involve her with other relatives. He had asked his cousin Flo to send him a *Gregg Shorthand Dictionary* and urged Ruth to follow up. While she was at it, she could ask Flo to send him some fudge because "she can make swell stuff." Other letters are peppered with his references to aunts and cousins whom he wrote about as if Ruth, too, were related to them.

Bob tried to reach out to Ruth's family as well. He was now only about one hundred miles from where her brother Ebert was stationed and promised to look him up—"I'm sure we could get acquainted very easily." Bob had also written to her brother Gordon.

Brother Ira received attention too. In a letter dated October 27, 1941, Bob asked Ruth to "take out 10 or 20 bucks for Ira's wedding present." By return mail Ruth shot back: "I don't really think you should give Ira anything—after all you hardly know him long [having] only seen him once." I was struck by her exceptionally rapid and brusque reply. I don't think she was trying to relieve Bob of an unreasonable expectation. More likely she was uncomfortable with his getting so involved with her family. In the end Bob compromised and sent a card. He also persisted. When he learned that the newlyweds had settled in San Diego, he asked her for Ira's address. If he got a short leave, he wrote, he might visit. As I later learned, he did.

A week after Bob arrived in Port Townsend, he learned that the training period was to be cut from three months to three weeks. The unexpected change got the rumor mill rolling: "We're scheduled to go out Wed to replace those missing on the 'Rueben James' that was hit a couple of days ago." A German submarine had sunk the destroyer while it was escorting a convoy in the North Atlantic; of the 159-man crew, only forty-four had survived.

When reality trumped rumor, Bob and his fellows didn't replace those killed on the *Reuben James*. Instead they departed for Treasure Island in San Francisco Bay. Created from a rock outcropping for the Golden Gate International Exposition in 1939, the tiny island boasted walled courtyards landscaped with thousands of exotic plants, the four-hundred-foot Tower of the Sun with reflecting pools, thrill rides, ferry slips, and a twelve-thousand-car parking lot.

By the time Bob got there, the U.S. Navy had transformed the state-of-the-art entertainment and exhibition venue—the exposition had displayed $20 million worth of artwork in three large halls—into a naval base with an airstrip and a personnel processing center. During the war processing personnel became its main mission; in those four years 4.5 million men passed through Treasure Island.

Though it was focused on keeping the conveyer belt moving, the base served other military functions as well. All sailors wounded in the Pacific Theater were shipped to its hospital, which, though small and understaffed, was never quite overwhelmed by the volume of casualties. Harbor patrol units, coast watchers, mine patrol forces, and tenders of antisubmarine nets called the base home, and it served as a docking station for the Moffett Field–based squadron of antisubmarine blimps. Treasure Island was also host to the Advance Naval Training, Fleet Operation, and Radio Operation schools. All in all, a busy little spot.[2]

Bob's second new home within a month was "much different than Townsend" and posed new challenges. With lights-out at ten, navigating the pitch-dark barracks after returning from work could be hazardous. Ants attacked food left in his locker and sand fleas bit him. Bob also faced the challenge of new social arrangements he deemed complicated, with "Marines—Navy—Army + everything on this blooming island," an island smaller than a square mile. At the height of the war the mess hall served as many as eighteen thousand men in two-hour stints, and its shopping list vividly reveals the scale of the human torrent roaring through Treasure Island. Each day 4,000 pies, 5,000 pounds of fresh bread, and 50,000 doughnuts were plopped onto trays; every meal required 200 gallons of gravy, 300 gallons of soup, and two tons of steak. The island bulged to a population of sixty thousand sailors and civilian employees, not counting more than a thousand German prisoners of war.[3]

As Bob ventured farther away from the base, he found yet another different world, as he described when he and two others "went over to Frisco and went to the hospitality house, nothing doing there so we just walked from 8:00 to 2:00 in the morning. Went thru all the dives and just looked—Sure were a lot of soldiers and sailors, thousands of 'em." Added to the strangeness

The *San Francisco Call-Bulletin* published this picture on October 12, 1945. The caption read: "The chow line is long but it moves fast and the food comes off the steam table piping hot and attractively served. There are eight steam tables in mess hall and each one handles between 900 and 1,000 men an hour. Mess hall crew is on duty 24 hours each day." Photo used by permission of San Francisco Historical Photograph Collection, San Francisco Public Library

of the city's preparations for war was the strangeness of the city itself: "Hiked all thru Frisco even thru Chinatown—Sure was dark and foreign. Went down thru the International Settlement. Sure got foggy about 12 o'clock. Could hardly get to see our way home."

I thought of my own experiences of culture shock. As a college student in 1974, I conducted anthropological research for a summer in Chuuk in the Federated States of Micronesia. I lived in the luxury of tiled flooring and screened windows with a Chuukese family, tried my best to develop a taste for pounded breadfruit and canned meats, and fumbled with the language, trying to immerse myself in the culture as much as I could. Yet, even with a year of preparation beforehand, I was unprepared for my feelings of alienation. Chuukese life challenged my most basic assumptions—about time, about social relationships, even about life itself. When I returned to Chuuk almost a decade later for a year of doctoral research, I was more prepared for the challenges of living in a different culture. I learned what to expect but every so often understanding still eluded me. Now, reading Bob's letters, I tried to imagine how he came to terms with his own challenges of culture shock. Perhaps, like me, he learned what to expect and that was enough.

"Your Picture"

By the 1940s snapshots had surged in popularity. Everyone seemed to clamor for a camera, taking pictures on special occasions or for no reason at all. Getting film developed required only a stop at the neighborhood drugstore; after just a few days shutterbugs could see how the pictures had turned out. Servicemen posted glamour shots of movie stars like Ava Gardner or Betty Grable in the barracks, while those who had a girl back home carried her picture on them and often, like Bob, showed it to everyone. "The boys seem to think you're especially nice lookin."

After just two and a half months in the service, "those pictures are almost worn out now. If you get any picture of yourself I'd like to have one or should I say two such as one on each side of a folder about the size of 4" or 5" square. That would be a nice size." About three weeks later, Bob got what he asked for, "a swell picture. Have been showing it to all the chiefs and shipmates."

That proved only the beginning. "I think I've showed everyone in the barracks your picture, I just don't know how to thank you

In a letter dated January 9, 1942, Bob wrote that he kept this picture of Ruth in a leather-bound case under his belt. Ruth was twenty-one when it was taken. Photo by Gene Garrett

and tell you how much it really looks like you. Just a spitting image. Showed it to the Executive Officer. " "Gosh," Bob continued in another letter, "I can't get over your picture, just everything's like you, eyes, hair, lips—everything's perfect——Boy Oh Boy, the fellas are sure getting eyefuls. The Exec claims I'm losing too much time looking at your picture. Cuz see, I carry it inside my belt. You don't realize all the places you have been (in picture)."

Having a picture of Ruth provided more than a way to remember what she looked like. Showing it around boosted his stock with others, including officers. The more beautiful the woman, the more manly the man. As men beheld Ruth's beauty, Bob could bask in reflected glory.

However, this could backfire: "Was telling the boys about you around here when I showed your picture and one of 'em asked me if I didn't feel inferior when I was with you or when I thought about you. But I don't." Yet what would happen to his image if Ruth left him? What would this say to his mates about the strength of his manhood? And about his ability to keep his girl? Brandishing her picture involved risk.

For now, though, the picture served as a visible connection to Ruth. He would "kiss your picture good night and call it a day." If he was feeling lonely, "all I got to do is look at your picture for a couple of minutes and everything's o.k. again." When he "studied your picture for quite a while," he felt like he "could reach out and say, 'Kiss me darling.'" Ruth's picture let him conjure her presence.

"All I Do Is Eat, Work, Sleep, and Dream of You"

Shortly before Bob had left Port Townsend, he had applied for the rank of yeoman. In the 1940s Coast Guard, a yeoman performed typing, stenographic, and clerical duties, including preparing reports and maintaining records. He maintained the filing system, furnished information on personnel matters, and recorded court-martial proceedings. Proficiency in shorthand was required for the rating of yeoman first class (hence his request for the shorthand dictionary). If Bob could win an office post, he would avoid more dangerous assignments like convoy duty. And since yeomen were assigned to recruiting offices across the country, he hoped the promotion might permit a return to Minneapolis.

After several weeks of working the system, Bob wrote that "the break has come"—he had been promoted to yeoman third class.

Bob (left) and an unidentified buddy socializing in their dress blue uniforms in San Francisco, perhaps celebrating Bob's February 17, 1942, promotion to yeoman third class.

The excitement of future possibilities took hold: A first-class rating "would mean close to $100.00 per month and allowances for board + room." He also hoped "to go up to district pretty soon," that is, the navy nerve center for the entire region.

Yet, once in the office, Bob found himself swamped. Working there was intense, pushing him to focus on his shorthand "almost continually." "We sure are busy," he wrote, "working every night to around ten o'clock. Am so busy I hardly have time to think." "Another twenty fellas coming in from Port Townsend, Washington, this coming Sunday which means some more work for us. More fun." After working one night until eleven, well after lights-out, he could hardly make it to his bunk. Still, the relentless pace continued—"All I do is eat, work, sleep, and dream of you, (from taps to revellie)."

I imagined that Bob now found himself experiencing a different kind of shock, war shock. Safely ensconced in an office, he processed the papers that sent "men or should I say kids" to places that would soon become major theaters of war. "New guys comin in and going out all the time. The Navy is sending 'em on merchant ships as soon as they can man them with guns." He participated in this vast effort to get as many men mobilized as quickly as possible. But he wasn't one of them. He remained out of harm's way, thousands of miles from the first battle.

But his situation could change. On November 21 he wrote: "There are 20 more C.G. men comin in Sunday morning and we expect a draft of 25 C.G. men to go to Hawaii. Hope I'm not in it." And then five days later, after they shipped twenty more men out to Honolulu, he breathed a sigh of relief: "Glad I didn't go."

But what did he feel on December 7, I wondered, when Japan attacked Pearl Harbor and war was finally declared? He had processed papers for hundreds who had been sent there. How did he navigate his feelings—the relief that he hadn't been there, the guilt that he remained in San Francisco?

I couldn't expect to find Bob's answer to that question, but I did find what he wrote of his experience that day:

Well, to start with the War, you know, the thing we're all in, (up to our necks) and we don't care much about. I was over in Frisco and some Dog faced soldiers came up to us and asked if we were from Alameda Base, Of course we weren't as we're from Treasure Island. So we didn't think much about it and a little further along I'd say about two o'clock everybody told us to get back to our stations. We, of course, didn't hurry much cause they don't have much in the line of extra duty or dirty work that they could sentence us to so ate a good meal before we went back, getting back to the island about five o'clock. They already had sentries every 500 yards for a period of 3 miles so we couldn't ride down, Had to walk all the three miles. When we got down to our quarters we were immediately mustered to go out all night over to Frisco and Oakland to help the F.B.I. round up all Japs who were suspicious.

The seizing of people of Japanese ancestry—racist, unjust, unjustifiable—was part of the fear and panic that gripped the area. By afternoon the army's Western Defense Command had received a report that a Japanese fleet loomed thirty miles off San Francisco's Golden Gate. The army issued shovels to every available soldier with orders to dig trenches on the bluffs facing the ocean.

With leaves and liberties "a thing of the past" and "no christmas presents forthcoming as we're all clamped down," Bob wrote to Ruth: "Don't know where I'll be from now on so please don't be disappointed or should I say disgusted with my not riting." No one could know what might happen next.

"I'll Never Never Get over It"

Bob also wrote of feeling "something really deeper" but understood that Ruth may not have felt the same way. "If there's any doubt in your mind," he stood ready "to clear it up when I see you next." Of course, with all leaves canceled the next time they would see each other could be a long way off. So he galvanized himself to infuse his letters with all that he could to bring Ruth closer, trying to address every possible threat to his love. It was a path fraught with anxiety. Since so few of my mother's replies

IT CAN—IT HAS HAPPENED HERE

It not only can happen here, it HAS happened. First San Francisco firm to protect itself against air raids is the Pacific Telephone & Telegraph Co., which has built a two-story fortification of sandbags around the building. U. S. sailors stand guard.

EVERYBODY'S WAR F.R. STRESSES Berlin, Rome

Bob enclosed this picture, torn from an unidentified local newspaper, in a letter to Ruth describing his experiences on December 7, 1941. In it Bob (noted by arrow) stands guard at the Pacific Telephone & Telegraph Company in San Francisco several days after the attack on Pearl Harbor.

survive, I couldn't determine how she responded to Bob's concerns. Did she write that she loved him? Stationed so far away, how could he know?

No wonder, then, that Bob depended more and more on Ruth's letters. Since they were "really what keeps me going," he urged her to "keep your letters coming." Yet letters could take him only so far, and he worried that "it would almost floor me if I was playin second fiddle." He promised that "as soon as I get out I'll be every much the guy you thought I was (if you did) and maybe more" and then waxed prophetic: "I love you so much I'll never never get over it. You're too much of an ideal—Hope you're conception of ideal is the same as mine."

My heart went out to my father. Here he was, pouring out his love to Ruth while worrying that he might be losing her. I suspect that my mother wasn't forthcoming about her own feelings. That would explain why his anxiety seemed to escalate with each letter. The more she held back, the more he expressed concern about her faithfulness, leading him to write ever more passionate expressions of undying love.

I began to see this pattern play out in the letters themselves. Bob's letters often started boldly. On December 12, for example, he responded to Ruth's expressing doubt about whether she loved him: "Give my picture a great big Kiss, take a long look, tell me that you love me, and then try and believe you aren't in love with me. I'll bet you can't." But then came the nervous add-on: "If you can please be sure and let me know."

More typically, though, his letters reflected an eroding confidence. He put himself among "a lot of disappointed guys if their girl friends at home go back on 'em." His anxiety required near-continuous bolstering. After he did not receive a letter for two days, he wrote, "I'm almost beginning to believe you've forgotten all about me." At one point he was blunt: "Been stepping out lately?"

The advent of 1942 didn't change things. On January 9 Bob responded warily to Ruth's report that she was looking for a platonic friend in Minneapolis: "I spose it's all right," he conceded, "but I'd hate to have you going out with any fella cuz you're just a little bit too good looking. I'm afraid I'll lose you if you start roaming." So he exhorted her to "be good and don't befriend any boys who look or act lonely cuz it isn't being done out here and I know you wouldn't want to start anything new, would you?"

But Ruth was dating. "Too bad I look so much like Johnny," Bob quipped, "but I'm glad I'm not like Bill." Ruth responded: "I'm so lonesome for you—or am I thinking 'bout Bill. Oh gee no—it's you this time." I hoped that she was joking.

Ruth wrote in early February that she had dated an intern. Bob replied, sarcastically I believe, that he was glad to hear about it. The news could only have exacerbated the worry that had filled his letters for months: "Hope you aren't going out too much cuz then I'll have competition." "Hope you're enjoying your work as much as ever—Are all your men patients just as amorous?" "I hope that no one's teaching you to like French kisses. If they have, I'll really have cause to start worryin. Or did you say you never went out?"

Meanwhile, after Bob and his fellows had suffered a month of severe movement restrictions by day and monotonous blackout conditions by night, liberties were reinstated. Even so, Bob continued feeling blue, and his restlessness about Ruth continued to irritate. He went out for a night on the town to blow off steam.

At mail call the next day Bob received a letter from Ruth. Since conditions in crowded barracks led him to destroy her letters, I don't have this one. But I do have his response. Apparently she had written of not understanding how he could be so sure of his love for her when she wasn't sure of her love for him, especially if he had taken up drinking and smoking. If he had, she warned, she would "lose faith" in him.

Bob shot back: "Honey, you know how I stand on things like that. I know you probably think I'll change but I'm afraid you're going to be wrong. I've got too many good reasons." He explained: "You're the first girl I've met who was a real girl and that who knew what she wanted and didn't want. I've made up my mind that you're the only girl for me. I know you question how I can be so sure but it's the thinking I'll have to explain to you when I see you." Later in the letter he reflected: "In re-reading page one it seems that I've taken the attitude that I've become quite possessive, please forgive me if I have." Even so, "I hope you realize how I feel, some day."

I could see from these exchanges that Bob didn't know Ruth very well. He had yet to learn that she struggled mightily about what and whom she wanted. Also, he didn't realize that she would need to have a say in his decision that "you're the only girl for me." And I could see that unresolved issues were starting to pile up. Bob seems to have felt so, too, for he often asked Ruth questions. When she wrote, for example, about a weakness that she had been trying for three years to overcome, he asked about it.

He enclosed that page of her letter and underlined Ruth's sentence with two red lines—"I wish [Veronica] could help me try to overcome my main weakness—I've been trying for about 3 years now"—and then printed in the margin, again in bright red: "What do you mean? Please xplain!" In a postscript he pleaded once more: "Please answer my questions, honey." I found no evidence that she did.

Bob interpreted Ruth's reticence as lack of certainty about whether she loved him, so he wrote on January 23 that "we'll just quit writing and wait 'til you want to come out and see Calif. and maybe then I'll be able to make up your mind for you." I was struck by those last words. Apparently Bob figured that Ruth was incapable of making up her own mind.

No sooner had he written this than he reversed himself: "Have thought it all over again and decided that we keep rite on riting." He ended with his customary worrying that Ruth might tear her hair out "at all the foolishness that I've written." His bold attempt to clarify whether Ruth loved him ended when he backed down again.

Once more my father's desperate uncertainty moved me. Admittedly he was young and infatuated. And his blistering work schedule only worsened his already frayed nerves. But even after factoring all that into his actions here, I didn't recognize him. He

I found out what she's really like.
Poor kid - if only she didn't have
such an eye for the men but that
must be her special weakness and
temptation to overcome. The next few
weeks will be hard for her and me
both because she'll depend on me
to help her along and I can't let her
down so I have to try my best to find
things to keep her occupied and in
that way help her to forget him. We
each have our little tasks to do along the
way, don't we? I wish she could
help me try to overcome my main
weakness - I've been trying for about
3 years now. 'S funny how we all
know our own faults as well as we
know our names but we have one
heck of a time trying to overcome them
and improve. I spose it's that way
all thru life. If we ever thought

Please explain! ← what do you mean?

was supposed to be a take-charge kind of guy, not hesitant and fretful. I didn't like to see him this way.

Then Bob met Ruth's father, Werner, in San Francisco. Everything about this meeting is strange. What would have brought a small-town preacher across the country during wartime in the middle of winter? And how could he have afforded the trip—especially a room at the Hotel Sir Francis Drake, an elegant downtown hotel? Even what Bob wrote about the meeting was odd. On stationery from the hotel he wrote "while talking with your dad." Though they talked about "lots of things," he mentioned asking only "whether you were getting fatter or not," and Werner replied that "you stayed the same." This is all that Bob wrote about the meeting; Ruth apparently wrote nothing. I hesitated to read into her silence, yet I wondered if she had not wanted Bob to meet her father because it would signify a more serious relationship with Bob than she desired.

Meanwhile, according to Bob, the uncertainty of their relationship continued: "Sure would knock my props out from underneath me if you ever rolled me over. But it would hurt lots more if you didn't let me know if you'd changed your mind." And two months later he again wrote that Ruth was "saying something in your letter about your tongue just not being able to say certain things. I was almost all set to give up but heck we can talk it over later. I was really pretty surprised. I still love you very very much and hope the feeling is mutual."

Bob's choice of topics didn't help to stabilize the relationship. For example, in a letter two days after Valentine's Day 1942, he reported to Ruth that he had received a telegram and box of candy from Madeline last Christmas, so he sent her candy for Valentine's Day as "just a diplomacy measure." Then he admonished: "Now don't you start any diplomatic gestures with any of the service boys or any boys for that matter cuz I may not understand how to take it."

Was Bob aware of his double standard? Ruth seems to have pointed it out and not just about Madeline: "You tell me not to get too friendly with the 'gals back home.' Don't you worry about that, honey child, cuz that would never happen." Madeline and Lill, another woman to whom he had written, are "both going steady with fellows already (so there)." Then he signed off: "Hope you're still being a good little girl and still sayin no just like I am."

Bob may not have been dating, but his night on the town back in January returned to haunt him. According to his service records, a routine physical exam disclosed that he had gonorrhea. The physician briefly described the incident that yielded the infection: "Last sexual intercourse was about 1-7-42, patient had been drinking with a pick-up girl in San Francisco." He was given three days of sulfanilamide, the standard treatment then, and remained on duty.

The letters don't say what happened. Based on how Bob described other liberties in San Francisco, here is a likely scenario:

With thousands of military personnel in the Bay Area, every restaurant, bar, and nightclub was jammed. After some searching, Bob and a couple of buddies found a bar with room enough to squeeze in. Then a young woman sidled up to Bob and asked, "Hello, sailor! Want to buy me a drink?" Bob was struck by how much the woman looked like Ruth. With each drink the resemblance grew stronger. When he and his buddies decided to leave, the woman whispered, "Want to come to my place?" And he did.

The family lore about my father when he was young prepared me to find evidence of his wildness in the letters. But I was unprepared to feel my own surprise. I suppose an unexamined childish denial explains it. As his son, I didn't easily imagine him having sex at all, even in marriage. Or perhaps it was his infection with a venereal disease. He could be wild, I figured, but *that* wild? The revelation exposed my naive belief that he should be invincible.

"It Sounds Too Good to Be True"

On March 25 Bob dashed off a note to Ruth about "a kid from Mpls who had been with me since I came down" and who had been killed in a truck accident. This death brought Bob an unexpected opportunity—to escort the body to Minneapolis. It sounded "too good to be true. In fact, when I start writing about it I get so shaky just in case I may lose out." Shaky or not, three days later he left for Minneapolis.

Bob's stay there couldn't have lasted long, given the "830 AM APRIL 3" postmark on a card sent from Wyoming on his return trip. Any time they spent together had to be sandwiched into the time available beyond the rigors of Ruth's nursing program. If her day off didn't coincide with his visit, unless Ruth played hooky they likely found just a few hours to spend together.

When he returned to Treasure Island on April 4, Bob found three letters from Ruth awaiting him and wrote late that evening: "If I'd seen that line where you stated you'd greet me in open arms I'd really [have] taken you at your word, but I didn't want to embarrass you or make it appear difficult so I, as you noticed, just stood like a rummy and said hello." His concern not to make their greeting difficult had arisen out of respect for members of the deceased serviceman's family who were at the station when Ruth approached. "Now that I'm back," he continued, "and everything is going swell, Mr. Vernet asked why I didn't stay over Easter." Bob had followed orders so sedulously it never occurred to him, as it had to his commanding officer, that he could have stayed longer. When I read that, I admired my father's single-minded diligence.

That diligence reminded me of when my father first told me that he hoped to get an airplane hangar built for Northwoods Air-Lifeline, a nonprofit organization that he and my mother founded to provide free air transportation for people who needed medical treatment unavailable in Michigan's Upper Peninsula. My reaction had been, "Dad, you're crazy. How are you going to raise that kind of money in the UP, where it's so poor?" But he did and a hangar was built. I ate crow and was proud of him. I hope I told him so.

As for that April 1942 visit, months after Bob returned from Minneapolis he reminisced to Ruth that "it was almost like we had to get to know each other all over again." And his recent treatment for gonorrhea—he probably didn't tell Ruth about it—could have inhibited his desire to show physical affection. No wonder he noted that it had been a "peculiar situation" when "I was pretty lax on loving you." He laughed at himself when "in the back of that hamburger shop" he was "so clumsy."

Their brief visit did nothing to ease Bob's anxiety about other men in Ruth's life. He had been back only ten days when he asked, "Who was it that left a message last week that you talked about in your letter?" Later he asked, "How's the Doc coming along?" Then the next day he wondered if she had "been corresponding with Bill in Chicago—(or anyone else?)." Ruth herself may have been asking Bob similar questions, for his letter ended by referring to their agreement not "to let anyone get you down no matter how easy it is to let yourself go—please—."

Easy indeed. Given its postmark, this letter from a man named Mac likely arrived in Ruth's mailbox even while Bob was in Minneapolis:

Gee kid, but I hated to leave there Friday afternoon. I sure would have liked to have had at least one more k—?? before I left, but when + if you do come out I'll expect to get one then. Thanks for the letter, but you forgot to send a picture in it, but you'll do that next time, wont you? I don't know what hit me, but I am afraid I fell pretty hard for you + I am not no kid no more, so I know what I am doing when I say I like you to darn much for my own good. I have a feeling that you think it is just a passing fancy with me, but believe me kid it isn't. I wish you felt the same way, but maybe some day you will. Say, when are you comeing out + then we can talk this thing over a little better + maybe we can sneak a few good kisse's?

    X just before you go to bed
    As ever

Mac

This letter bothered me. Ruth had been intimate enough to exchange kisses with Mac while extending her affection to Bob. In my dating years I believed that to be romantically involved with more than one woman at a time would be unethical. Here was my mother, though, practicing a thoroughly different ethic. This left me both surprised and confused.

On the envelope of Mac's letter, Ruth scribbled her typical notation: *Answered*. Was she playing the field, cultivating a dating life more active than even Bob had feared? Was she simply answering out of a dutiful sense that every letter deserved an answer? Or was it a little of both? Whatever the case, I now had to modify my unexamined lore about my mother's dating life. My assumptions from childhood—therefore naive—were under assault, and more was to come.

After Bob returned to California, he fussed to Ruth about why "you didn't commit yourself while I was home. I was getting kind of scared some other things had come up that you didn't want to tell me about." Their time together had not restored his confidence. Instead Bob bluntly asked: "Has someone or something else come up while I've been gone?" He denied that he was "losing faith" and speculated that maybe Ruth had been "afraid of hurting my feelings so you didn't want to tell me. Is there anything to that theory?"

Those long silences from Ruth, or at least silences that seemed long to Bob, continued. During one Bob was about "to regret all the things I've ever done." But a "surprise letter changed a lot of things." His response suggests that Ruth had come on strong, probably writing about how much she loved him. Her letter alleviated his worry—at least for now.

Then Bob had another reason to worry. He was hospitalized for eighteen days to treat "Gonorrheal Urethritis, acute." The sulfanilamide used initially to treat the infection had been ineffective, a common outcome in the days before antibiotics.

Venereal disease among servicemen was a constant problem. In an effort to address it, Congress, for example, passed legislation in 1941 forbidding houses of prostitution near military bases. In December of that year Bob had proudly reported that only two out of 197 in his unit had been restricted for venereal disease.

About his own springtime illness, Bob wrote some of the truth—that he was in the hospital—but not the whole truth—why he was there. He didn't write about the gonorrhea, nor, apparently, did Ruth probe for clarification. His service records confirm that on April 25 he was discharged from the hospital "fit for duty."

Meanwhile, a few days before that discharge, Ruth received a letter from another man. Chuck wrote of trying to contact her by phone but "came to the conclusion that it was happless, so I thought I would try writing a letter. I hope that you kids didn't get in any trubble that Saterday night, because that would have spoiled a swell evening. Don't you think?"

On the envelope of this letter Ruth wrote *ans*. She had been corresponding with Mac and now Chuck. A week later she received a postcard from yet another man, Stu: "Hope you're learning to like St. Paul by now. How do you like the hills to climb—good reducing exercises for you, or shouldn't I say that. Well, spring finally looks to be on the way—all the countryside seems to be awakening Tra-la-la!"

A passing comment in a later letter from Stu noted that he had previously dated Ruth. After she met Bob, Stu had turned his attention to Ruth's friend Veronica. Ruth wrote to Bob about Veronica and Stu, and Bob responded that Stu must be "plenty vain" and "get[s] around quite a bit." Bob advised Ruth to "tell her to drop the guy."

Then Veronica wrote to Ruth that she had broken up with Stu. I wondered what the postcard would mean to Ruth now. Did she see it as an indication that Stu wanted to come back to her? Whatever she thought, all she mentioned to Bob was the break-up with Veronica.

"So Don't Disappoint Me!"

In the middle of May, Ruth broke another period of silence toward Bob by suggesting that she visit him in California, perhaps within two weeks. Excited by the news, he shifted into high gear. He got approval for a ten-day leave, went to Los Angeles and picked up his cousin Arv's car, and scraped together $50—nowadays that would have been more than $700. He arranged for Ruth's lodging, suggested that she "bring my portable radio along," and instructed her to "call me, day or nite, as soon as you get in town."

After almost two weeks of feverish preparation, everything was ready and Bob was flying high: "Well, Baby, if I don't see you I'll really be very disappointed. So don't disappoint me!"

Then this telegram, dated June 1, arrived: "CANT COME, DARLING. TOO MUCH INTERFERENCE. AM TERRIBLY DISAPPOINTED. WILL BE THINKING OF YOU ALL THE

TIME. WILL WRITE AND EXPLAIN LATER LOVE= : RUTH."
Bob's postcard reply was trenchant:

10 day leave arranged—
Automobile on hand—
Plenty of money on hand—
Accommodations made—
Weather perfect—
Lots of friends to meet—
Then—a telegram received—
Then—Blooey—lots of people
disappointed, (If you only knew)

Bob

I was sure that Bob included himself in the "lots of people disappointed." And I could see his anger reflected in the missing salutation, closing, and affectionate expressions. The double underlining pierces like a dagger.

Despite Ruth's promise to "explain later," no letter in the box mentions what interference had kept her from visiting.

"Gone with the Wind"

At first Bob tried to hide his disappointment, writing that Ruth's failure to show up "doesn't seem to bother me much." Later in the same letter, though, his words suggest otherwise: "All the money I had saved for when you came out is now 'gone with the wind.' Too bad you weren't the wind it went with." By the end of the letter he had reached a deeper level of honesty: "I was quite swept away as you were quite definite in all your letters, you know." He also lost considerable face: "The fellows were giving me the razz cuz you didn't show up," and "Boy, I'm having lots of explaining to do." But, "thinking it over," he took an about-face from his hurt to say that Ruth was "very very much on the right side" not to come. "Please forgive me for encouraging you in the idea, will you honey?"

I couldn't grasp what Bob meant. Ruth had snubbed him, yet *he* asked *her* for forgiveness. Perhaps he hoped to soften the impact of the previous lines, worried that she might be put off by his negativity. His asking Ruth for forgiveness struck me as yet another example of his lack of confidence in the relationship.

Even so, as he continued to get "really lonesome," Ruth still lit his fire when he read her "very amorous letters" that made him "feel really up and coming." He offered to "really show you when I get a chance" and hoped she would be "just as willing." By the end of the letter, as if recalling his hurt, he shifted abruptly and mocked that she might be "tired out" from all her dating, concluding with this barb: "Oh, that's right, you said you didn't go out much."

Sarcasm aside, Bob had good reason to agonize about Ruth's going out. She had sent him a "quite serious letter" that left him "very much surprised" to find her referring yet again to a date she had. Her report of refusing drinks led him to hope that at least she was "stayin away from the necking and petting end."

In subsequent letters Bob expressed his anxiety time after time: "Still love me honey? If you don't you're really going to disappoint me." "If you go head over heels about some cute kid then be all means try and remember your little swede boy friend." "How's the love life?" "Please don't go and fall in love with any Taystee Bread truck drivers."

I considered these anxious expressions to be an indication that, however strongly Bob felt he loved Ruth, he was growing increasingly troubled about whether she felt the same way toward him. Even mustering an upbeat observation that "ever since I left home I could trust you with anyone, anyplace" brought heartache, reminding him that "once your faith is lost then everything goes haywire. You can't raise a very solid friendship on suspicion and worry, can you?"

As Bob asked that question, he appeared to have reached a point where accepting responsibility for his own life had become increasingly important to him, especially after his bout with gonorrhea. On the form setting forth the diagnosis and its cause, Bob had signed a statement acknowledging "this disease is the result of my own misconduct."

I can imagine those words' burning themselves on his conscience; they may have haunted him during his brief trip to Minneapolis with the body of his fellow Coastie; they may have stood as a stark warning that future misconduct would jeopardize his Coast Guard career, let alone his hopes for a long-term relationship with Ruth.

Whatever the reason, after he completed his treatment the second time and tests came back negative, they stayed that way. Throughout the rest of his military career, his medical records reflect consistency: "No disease." I think Bob had turned a corner toward responsibility.

Bob's emerging sense of responsibility appeared to change his socializing. I compared his infectious one-nighter in January 1942 with this description of a much different night on the town six months later:

We were leaving a restaurant night club and as I held the door open for Hank and the rest to come through Hank made a remark about a girls shoes who was standing alongside the counter. She turned but instead of taking Hank up on his remark passed him like a dirty shirt and hooked her arm in mine and proceeded to walk me down the street. Gee, they really were more surprised than I. (Boy, am I ever conceited.) She suggested I buy her a drink which I agreed hoping one of the others would take her over. She had her mind made up that she wasn't going with anyone but me. When I took out my bill fold to pay for the drink I saw your picture (of when we first met) and I made up my mind that I was the last guy she was going to take along. I showed her your picture and she prompted me to accept one of hers which I am enclosing. I was looking at it this morning and it makes me feel pretty low to think a girl can be as lousy and forward as she was.

A month later Bob assured Ruth that "I'm still a good little boy." Meanwhile Ruth's correspondents continued to multiply. In a letter to her parents in early May, she mentioned that "Greg writes every day." Greg Anderson was a recent enlistee in the army, and the Andersons were friends of Ruth's family. During Ruth's next year of school, she would lodge in Mrs. Anderson's house. But writing every day? Was this the action of a family friend or did it signify something more?

In early July, Ruth also received a letter from Dan. After asking about Bob, he got down to business: "I'll be frank, I have greatly appreciated your friendship and enjoyed our times together very much, and I would like to keep track of you."

Thirteen days later Russ Kowalski took his turn. After small talk about "the old grind" and "the swell weather," he asked Ruth about tennis courts and suggested that they might have "a good game of doubles some nite when I get back." Russ closed: "If you find time I'd appreciate if you'd drop me a line."

By the end of July 1942 Ruth's correspondents included Bob, Mac, Chuck, Stu, Greg, Dan, and Russ—not to mention the men, such as "the intern," who were nearby and so didn't need to write. With so many men vying for her attention, Ruth lost track of Bob. He wrote that he had not "heard from you for quite a little while" and asked: "What's wrong?" In his next letter he wondered again, "Should I have reason to worry?" He then rationalized his anxiety by adding, "I spose you've got a good reason for not writing so I'll let it go for a couple of days until I start worrying." But he didn't wait that long, reminding her a day later that he hadn't heard from her. Perhaps Bob's nagging finally found its mark. Two days later he glowed about "the swell letter I got from you."

For the moment Ruth appeared to be keeping all her fires tended.

Since family lore was silent about my parents' courtship, I had been left to imagine a straightforward path: my parents dated each other; they fell in love; they married. Isn't this the way it is supposed to go? Isn't this what every child absorbs without words? I hadn't imagined my mother's dating life was so vigorous or my father's anxiety so pronounced. I would have to make still more room for what I didn't know about my parents during these years.

The summer of 1942 ended well for Bob. He was promoted to yeoman second class with a raise in monthly pay to $96. And then, barely two weeks later, he pulled an all-nighter and successfully passed the exam for yeoman first class. His ambition bore even more fruit when on September 1 he was transferred to the district office at Bay and Powell in the heart of San Francisco. "Boy, do I feel good."

But not for long. In two weeks, as about twelve thousand service personnel passed through the Gateway to the Pacific *every day*, reality set in—a relentless, seemingly punishing, reality. Bob's office, with dozens of others, processed this mass of humanity one by one, as he wrote in his next letter to Ruth:

160 men incoming today
130   "   "   tomorrow
170   "   "   next day.

That was 460 men in three days. For every one of them a yeoman had to complete multiple typewritten forms using a manual
typewriter and carbon paper without benefit of a word processor
or photocopier. This workload—tedious, stressful, relentless—
weighed heavily on Bob. And the uncertainty of getting a leave
bothered him even more: "This place is getting on my nerves."
He was "starting to take liberty every night" to try to relax, but
he still struggled with "my restlessness."

Though despondent, Bob didn't give up, as he relayed to Ruth
a conversation with his immediate supervisor "talking about how
busy we were so I asked him if I could arrange leave pretty soon.
Then he said 'Oh, I 'spose you want to go home and see your little
Swede Mama?' So then I told him I was almost ready to go over
the hill"—slang for going absent without leave.

That evening on his way to the barracks, Bob bumped into his
commanding officer, who assured him that he would approve a
leave. With hope rekindled—"Keep your fingers crossed, Babe"—
Bob's funk lifted. Getting more letters from Ruth helped too. By
mid-September he had received two letters that she "apparently
wrote while in a very good mood. You just be in that mood when
I hit town and we'll really have a swell time." Four days later "Bobbie" wrote to "Dearest Bunnie" that he had been granted a ten-day
leave. "Just can't wait to hold you in my arms.—And give you a
great big 'bear' hug—(Maybe bare)."

This time the anticipation paid off. His leave came through,
and Bob made the long trek from San Francisco to Minneapolis
and back. In later letters Bob reminisced: "When I was home you
and I were really walking on air." "You just sent chills thru me
when I held you close." "We certainly grew to know each other in
the short while I was home." They managed to spend an intimate
night together: "I'm most always a pretty sleepyhead when I just
get up in the morning. Except, of course, that night at the Ken-

wood then I wasn't sleepy, was I hon?" Bob concluded by noting "how much better we got along the second time I was home than the first time."

Oddly the most momentous event of the leave receives only scant mention in the letters. Despite all the anxiety and suspicion of the previous months, Bob and Ruth got engaged to be married. Ruth's relative Ardis reflected: "I was so thrilled to hear about your diamond, it surely was a surprise. I never believed you'd get one before me but some girls just seem to know how to handle the men."

"It'll Be June in No Time"

On the evening of his return to San Francisco on October 7, Bob wrote that already missing Ruth made him "feel a little punk." But the prospect of their future plans buoyed him as he concluded that "it'll be June in no time"—June 1943, that is, when Ruth would be graduating from nursing school and marrying Bob.

But June was a long way off. Right now Bob could hardly restrain his excitement: "I told the fellas about the ring and have been really congratulated." The next day he was still reliving what happened: "I'm sorry sugar, if I seemed to put you on inspection that night at the Gopher. I didn't mean to. I was just admiring you, every inch of you! I certainly am glad I made a pretty good impression on you just in a few days. Thank you darling for asking God's blessing on me. Gee, every song I hear reminds me of you," as "You Leave Me Breathless" and then "Thanks for Everything" wafted from the radio.

A week later Bob started to anticipate modifying wedding plans as "it's beginning to look like changes are inevitable here." Even so, he continued to bask in the afterglow: "Arv surely was quite elated over the engagement. I believe he loves you almost as much as myself." Bob also started to sign his letters with the exuberant "Your future hubby."

Then Ruth wrote that she had gone on a date.

Bob crashed. He decided to quit writing Ruth, but after a few days, when he began "getting a little lonesome," he confessed to her that "the only way I can get over it is to write you a line. So I broke down and wrote you this letter." He concluded, as long as she was going to go out with others, "I'd rather have you tell me about 'em." Even so, his sign-off shows their step backward. "Your future hubby" had regressed to "Your loving boy friend."

While Bob's letters showed his desire to continue with Ruth, he couldn't keep from weighing in about her dating, as he closed his letter on October 24: "Still like to be an engaged girl?" Then, a week later, wondering whether "you've forgotten me" because of "too much Burt," he wrote, "What was the date of that Saturday night I gave you the ring? That's one date that I'm going to remember"—and signed off with "All my love to my future wife."

Ruth's dating, though, continued to gnaw at Bob, as his sarcasm showed: "Was just thinking how you stick to the letter 'B.' You know, Bill, Burt + Bob, maybe a few more I don't know of too. But then it isn't so bad cuz I've always stuck to brunettes." In another letter on the same day the sarcasm continued as he praised her for "being a good girl (with Burt and so forth)." To Bob, "being a good girl" meant that she wouldn't, in the words of the popular song, "sit under the apple tree with anyone else but me." To Ruth the apple tree appeared big enough to include other men too.

As he reflected on Ruth's dates in a letter five days later, Bob took a more philosophical tack: "Boy, I can't get over how much I trust you (and love you). Of course, love + trust go hand in hand usually. They do where I'm concerned." Did his qualifications, "usually" and "where I'm concerned," suggest that, for Ruth, love and trust may not coincide? He couldn't be sure if she felt the same way, as his next sentence revealed: "Say sugar, how's Burtie coming along? No digs, darling, just wondering."

Had he known, Bob could have also asked Ruth how Stu was coming along. On October 30, Stu the traveling salesman—rejected by the army so still in the Minneapolis area—sent her a postcard. With Bob and Burt swirling about her mind, along with her other correspondents, the irony in Stu's closing would have been hard to miss: "How's your engagement coming?" In a postcard a week later, Stu hoped "to see you next week."

"He's a Wolf!"

Though Bob apparently didn't learn about Stu until later, Ruth did write to Bob at length about Russ. Bob was perturbed. On November 11 he responded by returning part of Ruth's disturbing letter, even though it "isn't polite to return letters." He did so because he felt it was "the only way I can put across what I want to say." Thus I held in my hands several rare pages from Ruth herself, annotated by Bob's red pencil.

> *but as he's a salesman. Has a good job but now he's going in the Army—in fact he was sworn in yesterday. He said (he was very disappointed) when he heard I had a ring, but he at least wanted to see* HOW BOUT YOU?

As might have been expected, her detailed description of Russ—"He's only 21—will be 21 in May—but everyone takes him for much older. Nice-looking kid but very quiet. He's out of town a lot as he's a salesman. Has a good job but now he's going in the Army—in fact he was sworn in yesterday"— provoked Bob: "OUCH!" "He's a wolf!" No wonder he teased her grimly: "'Just' a kid?" When she wrote that Russ was disappointed that she "had a ring," Bob pushed, "HOW BOUT YOU?" Despite the ring, Ruth continued, Russ "at least wanted to see me before he went. So I went with him."

Ruth went on to describe what happened next:

> *me before he went. So I said I'd go with him. We went to the State and saw "Now, Voyager" with Bette Davis and Paul Heinreid. Ate at the Gopher and then home. Was sure a swell show—these psychological pictures seem to be in the limelight now—it was on the order of "King's Row" I think. Maybe no one else thinks the same but I do. In one part he said, "I can't give you the moon" and she said, "But we still have the stars." Which is very true, isn't it, honey? Maybe can't have everything we want right now but we are plenty lucky at that and will maybe be together soon and then what more could we ask for. Wish it were real quick.*

We went to the State and saw "Now, Voyager" with Bette Davis and Paul Heinreid. Ate at the Gopher and then home. Was sure a swell show—these psychological pictures seem to be in the limelight now—it was on the order of "King's Row" I think. Maybe no one else thinks the same but I do. In one part, he said, "I can't give you the moon" and she said, "But we still have the stars." Which is very true, isn't it, honey? Maybe can't have everything we want right now but we are plenty lucky at that and will maybe be together soon and then what more could we ask for. Wish it were real quick.

Reading this, I was as stunned as Bob must have been. Here his fiancée was writing a detailed description about a guy she dated, reporting the date, and then expecting Bob to join her in appreciating the film she saw. What was she thinking?

Ruth continued: "Vernie and Marge started working at the hospital yesterday. They said it was good to be back but boy! they really had to work from the way they talked. Getting so short of nurses. Vernie ran into John the first thing and of course she went right up to him and talked all over him. Which is the only thing I don't like about her."

Ruth confessed to being tempted—"I worry for fear I'll get flirtatious like her"—but not yet succumbing—and then she told

Bob: "Spank me if I ever do." For Bob, it wasn't *if* she would become flirtatious; it was that she *already was*. To him her dates with Burt and Russ were proof enough.

Ruth continued: "When I sit here and look around I see many pretty girls go by—honestly some of these kids are just beautiful. Wonder how a guy can settle down on only one as they seem to be doing as there are so many engagements all the time. Boy, if I was a fellow I think I'd maybe give them all a whirl for a while and still I s'pose that's kind of silly, too. Since I'm not a fellow I guess I won't have to worry about it anyhow."

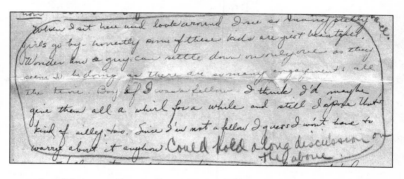

I saw her wondering "how a guy can settle down on only one" as expressing her own challenge in settling down with one man. Likewise, I took her speculation that "if I was a fellow I think I'd maybe give them all a whirl" as expressing her wish to date a variety of men. Perhaps this is what Bob had in mind when he circled the passage in red and wrote, "Could hold a long discussion on the above."

Ruth closed with "Be good now but have a good time while you can," which drew Bob's last response: "Just what do <u>you</u> mean?"

I shared Bob's demand. Did Ruth mean that Bob himself should go out with others to test the engagement? Or was she hoping that, if he did so, her own sense of guilt might be eased? Or did she assume he would be unable to "have a good time" after getting married, so he'd better have it now? What *did* she mean?

"A Four-Cornered Heart"

After Russ shipped out for army training, he wrote suggesting that his feelings for Ruth were growing deeper: "There's only one change I'd like to see in your life + I think you know what I mean. If that little matter shouldn't change + goes through before I get home please let me know will you. Because if I can't be the bridegroom I'd appreciate the privilege of being an usher any way."

"That little matter"—Ruth's engagement—didn't deter Russ from making a pitch for her. I couldn't tell how she responded; all I could go on was the *answered* that she wrote on the envelope. Four days later, in a letter relating some of his experiences in basic training, Russ changed his sign-off to *Love*. Again, she *answered*. A week later, in a letter reporting his transfer to another training station, Russ noted that he had left on such short notice that he wondered whether Ruth had answered his last letter, especially "whether or not you have a picture for me." Having one "certainly would break the monotony of this darned confinement." He again signed off with *Love*.

Ten days after that, Russ responded to a letter from Ruth. She had written something like "I bet you're surprised to hear from me again." Why would she have thought so? Because she hadn't written for a while? Or because she was engaged? In any event Russ started his reply: "Yes, I must say I was surprised, but I like surprises when they are as pleasant as this one." After updating Ruth on his latest training experiences, he got down to business:

> As for this marriage situation, I suppose I should be satisfied that I was lucky enough to have met you and to have enjoyed your company while I was in Mpls, but somehow I'm not. Ruth, I want you to know that I have a great deal of love and respect for you and I guess I'll just have to make the best of whatever fate has in store for me. And, as you say it may be a long time + many things may happen so I guess I still have a right to be an optimist + hope that something may happen in my favor. Haven't I?
>
> If I'm taking too much for granted I wish you would please tell me, Ruth as whatever happens after this thing is over I wouldn't want to spoil our friendship no matter whom you may marry, and you would still remain in my book as one of the finest persons I have ever met.

In another letter Russ wrote: "I guess I'll just have to wait till my time comes as you say. After all, I guess you're right in saying that our major concern right now is to win this war first." Again, he hoped the door remained ajar; at least she apparently wrote nothing to dissuade him.

Once more I could deduce part of Ruth's response from Russ's next letter: "I'm glad you have room for me in at least one corner of your heart but since when do you have a four cornered heart? I know it's unusually large but I didn't know they were making them with four corners these days."

Besides Bob, Russ, and Stu, I pondered who filled that fourth corner. Probably Greg. Now in the army, he still showed considerable interest in Ruth. In a letter to her parents she noted that "Greg writes every day," but in the same letter mentioned "Greg's girlfriend, Dorothy." Corresponding actively with each other while nurturing another romance, Greg and Ruth seemed to be well suited to each other.

Only a few of those letters survive. On November 20, two months after her engagement to Bob, Ruth accompanied Greg and his mother to see him off at the train station. He wrote: "I sure think a lot of you and only wish I had a better chance to 'get in there and pitch.' I hope someday I'll be able to. I sure wish I could see you again. I really miss you a lot, kid," and closed with "I love you Ruth + hope to be able to see you soon again or at least hear from you. All my love." On the envelope Ruth wrote *ans.*

I found no evidence that Ruth told Bob about her correspondence and meetings with Greg. Somehow—perhaps through the extended family grapevine—Bob knew enough to be concerned. In a letter on November 11, Bob included this postscript: "Don't be too good to Greggie, sugar!" And in a letter four days later: "Has Greggie come home yet? Just a little razzing honey."

As 1942 drew to a close, Ruth had created a challenging situation for herself. Though she had agreed to the engagement with Bob in September, she kept channels of correspondence open with other men, especially Russ and Greg. By refusing to disabuse them of their romantic aspirations, she put ever more strain on her engagement. Her relative Ardis seemed to reflect Ruth's quandary when she wrote: "Do you still kid the other boys too? The ring is inconvenient that way, isn't it. What did the other boys think? Another girl, gone wrong, I s'pose, huh?"

I was deeply troubled to learn of my mother's continuing relationships with other men while she was engaged. I had assumed that, once engaged, she would have remained solely committed to her fiancé. What left me flabbergasted, though, was the number of relationships she nurtured at one time. She reminded me of a song from *Oklahoma*, a musical popular at the time: "I'm Just a Girl Who Can't Say No." Not only could she not say no, it seemed, she wanted to say yes. This wasn't the mother I thought I knew.

What did being engaged mean to Ruth? I could have understood some youthful indiscretion here and there. But *seeking* relationships with numerous men—for many months—while she was engaged? Her actions showed a side of her that, even as I write, I still have trouble believing. Her behavior departed so sharply from the ethical standards by which, lore had taught me, she had always lived.

I mused about Ruth's status as the youngest in the family—a status that I shared. As the youngest I often felt the last to know what was going on. It was as if some party was happening somewhere but nobody told me where. Later, if I asked, the family was always surprised that I didn't or couldn't have known. It happened again and again; it still happens even now, in my middle age. As the youngest I got used to being left out of the loop and settled in at what felt like the family's margins.

A story about my youngest stepdaughter suggests that I'm not alone. One day the two older girls were reminiscing about a particularly luscious chocolate dessert—a rare treat of their rather ascetic upbringing. Laura listened for a while and then asked, "Where was I?" That childhood plaint, from a person not yet born at the time of the treat, echoes resoundingly among other youngests.

Was my mother's experience as the youngest similar? She never spoke to me about it. If it was, I can see her as not only the last to know about what was going on but also as the last one to be given any opportunity to choose, make decisions, or decide matters. And the situation may have been exacerbated because she was a girl while all four of her older siblings were boys. I can imagine their treating her condescendingly because, as the youngest, she needed to be told; I can imagine their treating her with little respect because, as female, she was seen as weak.

A 1942 letter from Ruth's brother Ebert shows this kind of relationship. Ebert was claiming her as a dependent, and he wrote of hoping to increase her allotment from $10 to $22 per paycheck. After giving her detailed instructions about how to determine and list her monthly expenses, he told her "the best way to handle things" if an investigator were to show up at her door. Through two long paragraphs he urged her to "tell [the investigator] what the facts are but be careful not to exaggerate them" and "if you are doubtful say 'I don't think so' or 'I don't know.' Don't lie but don't be too much the open book. I know you'd never lie but what I mean is don't incriminate yourself. You can say that you need more help from me now than before cause your Dad is unable to stand to much of the strain."

If family dynamics were like this, everything came to Ruth from above. Her parents set expectations and demanded that she meet them, but she would never have dared to demand anything from them. Her brothers could tease her, but she would never have dared to tease them. All of it—expectations, advice, censure—ended with her. Whatever the family expected in return would have been defined by this chain of command. Ruth would have had little say. She grew up with hardly any experience in making decisions.

I believe that this family dynamic shaped the template for Ruth's passive style of decision making. Upon her departure for college she left the circumscribed familiarity of her face-to-face community for the unrestricted anonymity of the giant university. If she hadn't developed confidence in making her own decisions while growing up, how could she be comfortable making them now? I can imagine her, debilitated by the fear of choosing wrongly, concluding that the best choice was not to choose at all.

Or, forced to make a choice, Ruth would second-guess herself endlessly. In my boyhood it always seemed to take forever to get her through one of those multiple-flavor ice cream parlors. She'd carefully scan each tub of ice cream and comment about the relative merits of each possibility. Even after she made the painstaking choice, she seemed unsure about it—might Rocky Road have been better after all?

I also had to remind myself that Ruth lived in a tumultuous time. Tossed from tiny Balsam Lake to the wider waters of the university, she found herself further buffeted by the waves let loose by the storms of war. Her life was chaotic and her grasp of her own circumstances was precarious. She was groping her way, and the way was far from clear.

Returning to my own dismay when I realized the extent of Ruth's dating life while engaged, I wondered how I had internalized the idea that being engaged meant fidelity to one person. Perhaps from Ruth's silence. She had been so effective at keeping her premarital relationships secret that I could, and did, absorb the fairytale ideal about engagement. Without an inkling that her experience departed so sharply from that ideal, I uncritically accepted the belief that engagement was between two people only. Now, once again, I had to address the difficult task of revising family lore.

Family lore, I found, is particularly resistant to revision. As a child I took at face value the stories my parents told me about their lives before I was born. I lacked the ability to ask clarifying or critical questions. Add to this my tendency to believe the best of my parents, and family lore became a formidable force indeed. Even well into middle age I find it difficult to incorporate knowledge that contradicts it. When I tried to understand my mother's actions in light of that lore, my cognitive dissonance irritated me. I didn't want to have to change what I had held dear for so many years. I didn't want to revise family lore.

So how do I deal with it? Perhaps I have to admit that my mother and I differed fundamentally about romantic relationships and what each partner owes the other. Or maybe emotional immaturity prevented her from knowing what she wanted from a relationship, so she tried out lots of them. Or maybe she used other men as comparisons to help her decide whether to marry Bob. I don't know. In the end *why* Ruth behaved as she did can't help me come to terms with her having *done* so.

When I reflected on what my mother did, I thought that the Ruth of these letters must have undergone a comprehensive change before she became my mother. But then I realized that I have little or no basis for that impulse. So much of her later life is as opaque to me now as her young adult years used to be. This leaves me wondering whether the mother I thought I knew was just a cardboard cutout. I'm not sure I knew her at all.

"All Future Engagements with Males . . . Will Necessarily Be Cancelled"

On New Year's Eve 1942, Bob wrote: "The orders are written and I'm so nervous now my stomach's starting to play tricks on me. Only about 12 hours to go before I shove off." Perhaps his stomach's antics reflected his mixed emotions. He longed for Ruth to see breaking news of another visit from him as a "pleasant surprise," but he remained uncertain. Although he was in a "happy mood," he admonished her that "all future engagements with males other than the immediate members of your family will necessarily be cancelled (of course you understand that)." Did she? Bob seemed to worry about whether she understood, and I certainly did.

The meeting seemed to go well for the couple. They were, as Bob wrote afterward, "almost in a trance." Even six months later memories of their time together remained vivid: "We really should've stayed out all night," and "Sleeping together is fun if you don't snore," and "I felt pretty blue myself when I left the station but am glad of it cause then I knew myself how deeply I felt for you." The highlight of the "perfect day" occurred "in the afternoon when 'we' tied 'your' legs in the telephone cord and later when you got your spanking. Quite a spanking, I'd say."

I had already had plenty of surprises about my parents' relationship. But now sadomasochism too? Probably not. In the 1940s romantic spanking was widely understood as flirtation. Superman, Batman, and other comic book heroes were among its most popular exemplars. In a 1941 strip, for example, having just undergone a sound spanking at Superman's hands, the "Blonde Tigress" Lil Danvers sighs dreamily: "Too bad he and I are foes—I could go for him in a big way."[4] How did Ruth feel about her own spanking?

Remembering those days left Bob feeling confident: "I'm under the opinion now that we'll do very very good—Now don't you say that we haven't known each other long cause you'll rate another spanking when I get home again, if you do."

But the afterglow of their January meeting cooled quickly. On the day Bob left, he spotted a framed picture of Ruth with another man. Eight months later, with the recollection of that experience still vivid, he recalled: "If it would've been any other time it probably would never've phased me but it certainly did that last time." By late March, when he hadn't heard from her "in so long that I started worrying," he finally received a letter the next day. But it didn't ease his worry. "In your long letter," he replied, "you spring a lot of things about the future I hadn't thought much about." Worst was his unhappy conclusion that she seemed to think "it would be better if we didn't see each other."

Based on other replies to Ruth's letters, I can be reasonably sure that she wrote about slowing down their relationship and postponing marriage until after the war. Bob responded with an unusual tactic: he intentionally refrained from writing for almost a week. Then, perhaps fearing that he might be losing her, he capitulated. After reporting what he had been doing each of the past five evenings, he was placatory: "Please don't be angry for not having rec'd a letter 'til now 'cause I didn't mean to let it go so long." For him a week was a long time; thus his apology. His next letter, though, reclaimed the high ground: "I'm sorry I have such a 'case' on you, sugar, but we'll have to really talk it over when we see each other soon."

Resuming his customary pace, Bob didn't take long to start probing again: "Am listening to a lonesome tune, 'I wish I had a sweetheart,' but it doesn't seem to bother me much cause I'm of the opinion that I do still have a sweetheart even tho she isn't here at the present time. Am I right, dear? Or is it just supposition?" And again: "Was just looking at your picture again and thought of how many different things a person thinks of when you're riting on a photo and forwarding to someone. On your's you have "With love Always Ruthie" Would it be the same now if you had to do over again? Oh—oh—Was I stepping on something I shouldn't have?"

I know her answer because he quoted part of it in his next letter: "'I will love you always—probably a little different than when I wrote that on my picture and maybe not the way you love me but I'll always love you in my way, honey.'"

"Love you in my way"? Bob blasted back: "Now just what's the explanation of the foregoing? Sounds plenty mysterious to me. Would appreciate if you'd pull me out of the dark." He may have been shaking his head a week later when he wrote that "there's so much about you that I just can't seem to get over honey." He wasn't ready to move on without Ruth, but neither was he confident in a future with her. Confused, he grew restless.

He considered a "transfer over town to the Beach Patrol head-quarters," but then "I would be like a darn civilian." Besides, beach duty "gets monotonous and under your skin sometimes," and it "would mean being in San Francisco indefinitely." Then Bob thought of going "aboard a ship," but he quickly dropped that option since "sea duty is time wasted too." He closed his musings by asking Ruth: "What do you think about it? I always like to hear how you feel about it."

Ruth's next letter seemed to provide a breakthrough for Bob. As she persisted in keeping her distance, and since it looked like the war would continue for some time, he decided that he may as well try officer training. With uncertainty enveloping his future with Ruth, what did he have to lose? So he talked to his personnel officer about getting the required sea duty to be in a position to submit his application.

The requested transfer came immediately. On May 8 Bob wrote his first letter from the USS *Eridanus*, a transport ship. Free from the office grind, Bob thought about asking for a leave when the ship arrived in Seattle because "you perhaps realize there are a few things that you and I are going to have to take care of." No sooner had he penned those words than he started another letter: "In the last 5 minutes my leave was cancelled and we're sailing again tonite—Boy—I'm really low but I'll get over it." With all leaves canceled, where was the ship headed? His postscript surmised: "They say 'Kiska' looks good in the springtime."

Kiska? I had never heard of it. I learned that in June 1942 the Japanese took control of that small Aleutian Island and immedi-ately started building fortifications. In October, American planes bombed the island. By the time Bob speculated that his ship might be sent there, a full-scale Allied invasion was thought to be im-minent. It didn't happen until August 17, 1943, when more than thirty-four thousand Allied forces, including ninety-five ships and

168 aircraft, attacked Kiska. But not a shot was fired; the troops found the island abandoned. Weeks before, the Japanese had evacuated under cover of heavy fog.

"You Can Imagine How I Think Something's Wrong"

Bob must have been relieved when he learned that in a few days the *Eridanus* would not go to Kiska but would return to San Francisco. Yet the loss of the hoped-for leave took him "really low," and not receiving a letter from Ruth "for almost three weeks" added to his funk. Not until five weeks had passed did he hear from Ruth, in a telegram that he read "about a hundred times." He had sought an assignment to sea duty when he felt that his future with her was bleak. Now her telegram offered hope that "we could [have been] seeing each other every nite, reading, riting, talking, and every thing together." As a result he was "kicking myself all over for getting on this 'garbage scow.'"

Because Ruth's message came by telegram, it must have been urgent. Had she proposed to visit him? Whatever the telegram said, its impact didn't last. A few days later, when he had heard no more from Ruth, Bob imagined that something was wrong. In a later letter, after reporting that a fellow yeoman in the office had married, he threatened: "Now don't you rite + tell me you've changed your mind."

By midsummer Bob was dreaming of being closer to Ruth when he returned from sea duty, perhaps before Christmas. But his fear of what she might do hounded him, snapping at the heels of his dream: "That is, if you don't go and get yourself married off a'fore I get back. Bert or Stu or someone—(Just kidding, dearest)." But he wasn't kidding. "If you do, be sure he's better than I am. So you can see, I don't worry." But he did worry. Beneath his bravado his hurt festered. And the longer Ruth kept silent, the more he felt that he had indeed lost her.

In the meantime a three-week public health practicum in a nearby town had offered Ruth more opportunities to expand her social life, as shown by this April 12 letter from Nick:

> I'll bet that you've about given up hopes of hearing from me by this time and have about definitely concluded with a sigh of relief that I'm just another small-town wolf who 'loves 'em and leaves 'em'?! Seems to me that it was just four weeks ago tonite that we took Fred back to school at De Pere—am I right? I can still picture you sleeping peacefully on the way home snuggled so cozily betwixt me and the steering wheel, and with your head resting softly on my "idle" arm. Gosh, but that was solid comfort! Talk about revolutionary methods of solving the sleep problem— that was it, and take it from me, gal, nothing could have kept me wider awake!
>
> I'm still recounting and reliving in my memory the times we spent together during your brief stay in our little city. How's about giving me the lowdown if and when you find yourself with a little time on your hands?

Two weeks later Ruth received this letter, on stationery of the local police department, responding to one that she had written to yet another man:

> Received your letter O.K. and was sure glad to hear from you, really thought you had forgotten me, but see you didn't, I really missed you after you left just can't get you out of my mind, to bad we didn't get out together sooner, I sure did enjoy it the night we were together even if I was nervous, you should be here now my wife has been gone for two weeks + is still away, so you see

how we could enjoy these nites if you were here, but you are not so guess all I can do is just dream of you which I do most of the time anyway.

It sure was funny the way we each liked one another + still thought the other one was spoofing, I like you so much that I just couldn't come out, + tell you + then have you make a fool out of me, I have never felt this way to any girl since I have been married. Well am not going to talk about it any more because it sure makes me lonesome for you.

Surely am sorry to hear you were sick, wish I could have been there to take care of you—also to tuck you in at nite + also give you a good nite kiss, but as is will just dream of it all, that is even nice if you cant have the real thing.

Hope this letter does not get on your nerves + hope I hear from you real soon, don't worry if you send them to Ray I will get them O.K.

Will close with love

Your crazy admirer.

What do you say when you learn that your mother, while engaged, spent a night with a married man and then wrote to him encouragingly afterward? At first I was appalled. Had she lost her moral compass? Then I reflected further. If someone came to me with a similar tale, as a pastor I would try to help the person understand what he or she had been looking for by engaging in such activity. And I would be as nonjudgmental as possible. As a son, though, I couldn't keep myself from judging my mother. Why? What is it about my relationship with her that elicited this response?

I reacted differently to Ruth's relationship with Russ, perhaps because she appeared to have genuine regard for him and he wrote respectfully. As she had done once before, she revived her correspondence, and he responded immediately: "Well, I must say I was surprised to hear from you again. No, I hadn't forgotten who you are but I <u>was</u> under the impression that perhaps you had forgotten me as I believe you did owe me a letter. Right?" After updating Ruth on his recent experiences, he concluded: "Don't forget you promised me some snapshots about a year ago. Remember? I'll be waiting for them."

About six weeks later Russ wrote: "By the way, you aren't married yet are you? It seems nearly everyone I know has been home on a furlough lately so I thought perhaps 'Bob' had been home too."

Russ's replies continued: "I just mailed a letter to you last nite, but thought I'd just write a few lines to thank you for the swell card anyway. I was rather surprised to get the card as I didn't remember telling you when my birthday was. Thanks a lot anyway. Here's wishing you all the luck in the world in whatever you decide to do Ruth. I'll be anxiously waiting to hear from you."

Stu continued to write when he traveled for business, as he did on April 19 when he sent Ruth a get-well card. On a note inside he chided her for her "fine way to get out of a date." Then he reported that "Don + I brought your radio + little pillow over last nite about six but the nurse at the desk was too tough to get by." What was Stu doing with Ruth's radio and pillow? Or was it Bob's radio—the one from the Lake of the Isles date and the one he had suggested she bring on the visit that didn't happen? Whatever the case, eight days later Stu wrote: "We'll have to have that bowling game soon—I want you to teach me!"

On his vacation in mid-May, Stu jotted a postcard: "Did you recover from the going over the pack of wolves gave you when we went bowling? Also did you sneak in without anyone awakening? Too bad I couldn't have come in and given you a good rub down! I had to go back and sleep with thin, little, Eddie! Gee, you were mean!"

Ruth also rekindled her correspondence with Greg, who replied on April 28:

> It sure was nice to hear from you again. Of course you know my feelings toward you and I know they'll never change. I can readily see your point in not getting married until after the war though. I forget how long you said you knew Bob before he entered the service but I'll bet it wasn't long enough. And I know in my case with Dorothy that we didn't know each other really well enough to get married and I saw no sense in getting married as long as we were so far apart. But I do think of you everyday, Ruthie, and when this war is all over with, maybe we can make some sort of decision. Right now we'll just plan on having a good time when I get home on furlough and otherwise a friendly letter now + then.
>
> I'm quite apt to be there about graduation time. I hope so anyway.

What sort of decision did Greg have in mind that he and Ruth would make after the war? To marry each other? And what kind of "good time" did Greg imagine? Whatever his intentions, Ruth wrote on the envelope "answered 5-23-43 late huh?"

Thus from March to June 1943 Ruth had corresponded with Nick, a "crazy admirer," Russ, Stu, and Greg. She had spent time with the two men from Clintonville, and she was dating Stu, Greg, and perhaps others, like Burt or the intern who lived locally and so didn't write. Bob was at sea, but he may as well have been on another planet. Ruth hadn't written to him in more than five weeks.

"I Certainly Hope All Went Well with the Graduation"

Then an unforeseen event made Ruth's future even more precarious. With her last term in nursing school over, she joined her classmates, family, and friends for commencement, where she received her bachelor's degree.

Or so they all believed. Ruth knew otherwise. Her grades for the last term included an incomplete for a class in child welfare and an F for a required sociology course. She had failed to complete her program. Without a nursing degree she couldn't be a registered nurse.

Family lore told me nothing of this. Since my mother had been valedictorian of her high school class, I had always assumed that she had been an excellent student. But her grades for her first two years at the University of Minnesota were only in the B- to C+ range. Worse, she self-destructed in her last semester and didn't earn her degree. But lore had her passing with flying colors, earning her nursing degree, and becoming a registered nurse. I was astounded to learn that what lore presented as a smooth path had been so bumpy and broken.

Ruth must have felt intensely ashamed about this failure. Astonishingly she told no one—not Bob, not her friends, not even her parents. Bob sent roses with a card: "I certainly hope all went well with the graduation." Stu sent his congratulations with a postcard from his vacation. Russ wrote his "congratulations. Here's wishing you all the luck in the world in getting a job that will keep you happy." And dozens of other congratulatory cards must have added to the weight of her shame. Again astonishingly she saved them all anyway. Maybe they helped her to fantasize that her graduation was real or at least that it might become real.

I would never have expected my mother to act like this. She made me hot cocoa on a cold day. She bought me nice clothes for school. She took care of me when I got sick. Sneaky and deceptive? No way. As I considered this new information along with that of her active dating life while engaged, though, it was increasingly obvious that my understanding of family lore about my mother was inadequate. I tried to make sense of her deceiving so many people. Perhaps she figured that keeping silent would buy her time to figure out what to do next—to try again to finish the degree requirements or to abandon nursing altogether. Whatever she was trying to do, with her active dating life jeopardizing her engagement and with her professional future so uncertain, her quandary grew.

Not only had my mother's life become a mess, but she was responsible for most of it. Before I read the letters, I couldn't have imagined ever writing those words. I had thought of her life as so tidy; she never got herself into a problem she couldn't solve; she never strayed from the right path. Now I wasn't sure what to make of her. Her actions represented the kind of behavior that I believed she would have abhorred and avoided. But here she was, it seemed, stumbling in deeper while covering her tracks.

Ruth had to move forward somehow. Friends and family assumed she had successfully finished her program. They also assumed that she would be getting a job, especially in wartime when nurses were in demand. And her parents were pressuring her to do so for financial reasons. So, not wanting to disappoint anyone and despite lacking the proper degree, she started to look.

"It Is Difficult to Make Up Your Mind About a Position"

Among Ruth's first inquiries was to Kay, perhaps a former instructor, who on June 15 thanked Ruth "for your nice long letter. I can well understand," Kay continued, "that it is difficult to make up your mind about a position." Then she reported about several insurance and public health positions "that no doubt would be available."

Others asked about Ruth's progress. Greg's sister June wrote that she "would like to hear how you came out with your state board." A month later Russ asked: "Have you started working yet?"

I don't know how Ruth spent the summer, except that she didn't do the work necessary to finish her nursing degree. The letters indicate that she continued to keep her academic failure a secret, so that if she told the truth now, she would have to face not only the failure but also her having been deceptive about it. Perhaps she hoped to find a nursing job of some sort without the truth's becoming known. That way she could later finish her program secretly.

Keeping the secret would have weighed heavily enough on Ruth, with ongoing parental expectations adding to the load. A lengthy letter from her father, Werner, for example, mixed paternal concern, parental nagging, pages of pastoral exhortations, and bits of worldly wisdom with a touch of sarcasm: "Your long expected letter came last nite. You must have been sick when you could not drop us a plain P. card to let us know how you was. You say you are tired so you can't write more. You must be quite weak. You left out 'thanks for sending $50.00 to Andersons' in your letter."

Werner urged her to "put yourself on higher ground" and to see her job as "service to suffering humanity for Christ's sake." He discouraged her from her plan to check out a job opening in Two Rivers, Wisconsin, noting that such a trip would lead only to "still more uncertainty," be a "loss of valuable time," and "a useless expense of money." In addition, "you would not have a free doctor and hospital at Two R." He exhorted that "there is not—believe me Ruth—any flowery path laid out for any of us in this world" and "to waste much more time on fence riding and daydreaming about the Green pastures on the other side is, as I have written you before, very detrimental." Instead he suggested that she consider the slogan that the Boy Scouts of America had adopted for that year—"Toughen up, Buckle down, Carry on to Victory"—and asked: "Would that be something that you need?"

Werner and Ruth's mother, Lilly, favored a six-month position at the university-affiliated Minneapolis General Hospital. They assumed it would allow her to make a "record there to refer back to, when applying for positions in the future." Of course, they had no idea that she wouldn't be considered for the position, as the university was well aware that she hadn't finished her nursing program.

Family lore about my maternal grandparents was necessarily mixed. Since Werner died when I was a toddler, what I knew of him came through photographs and rare anecdotes. His parents had died when he was a child, disbanding the family and motivating his emigration from Sweden to the United States as a teenager. He taught himself English and earned his divinity degree from the Swedish Baptist Seminary at the University of Chicago, where he met Lilly, who attended the nearby Baptist Missionary Training School.

After Werner's death Lilly came to live with us and remained until her death when I was sixteen. As boys my brother and I stayed with her in the summers at the family cottage in Upper Michigan, times that remain in my memory as the highlights of my childhood. When my mother went to work every day, Grandma remained reliably on hand when I got home from school. She cooked regularly for us, and in my imagination I can still smell her cinnamon rolls or rye bread baking in the oven. I knew her as a sweet-spirited woman, committed to her Christian faith in a soft-spoken way.

The letters confirm these memories. Lilly's exude tenderness yet reflect efforts to make peace between Ruth and Werner. As for Werner, his sensitivity is well hidden by the sternness of his oratory and his judgmental response to the little that Ruth shared. I understand better, reading his letters, how Ruth's behavior might have represented a rebellion against childhood strictures.

"I Can't Expect Any More Letters Than I Have Rivals"

Meanwhile Bob's summer passed at sea. Writing before he returned to San Francisco, he hoped "to have more than two letters for me when we get to port" and reverted to his customary worry: "But, of course, I can't expect any more letters than I have rivals, can I?" Ruth had written of dating two other men whom he called a pair because "a pair is easier to dispose of than two." Then he conjured up his own brand of wishful thinking: "Thanks, I knew you'd dispose of em. You're a darling that I'm glad no one has but me."

But Ruth didn't dispose of Bob's rivals. She wrote to them, as Stu acknowledged: "Received your cute little card to-day—thank you for your interest in my case, nurse!" And again, in a postcard two weeks later, he expressed a "hope to see you this weekend." A few days later Russ noted that "I just got your letter yesterday" and thanked her for sending "your invitations when I was down at Las Vegas. I got them just about two hours before the occasion was to take place. If I'd gotten them a couple days sooner I'd have been there. Well, I can dream can't I?"

Besides writing and inviting, Ruth cultivated her relationships with Bob's rivals physically, as indicated by Stu's inquiry in an August letter: "Did you find any hickeys on your [word scribbled out] or shouldn't I ask? If you did—I'll go sit in the corner and be a bad boy!" For the part of her body where Stu may have put those hickeys, Ruth used copious amounts of black ink to render that word indecipherable.

I paused. Did I really want to get into this? Had my curiosity given way to voyeurism? I reflected on Ruth's having obliterated only the offending word when she could have simply destroyed the whole letter. I think she kept the modified letter because it gave her a desirable memory minus the undesirable shame that she likely associated with a part of her body. This felt strange to me. It suggested a person for whom morality meant careful parsing. The intimacy itself was good; where Stu may have left evidence of it was bad. All the while, the bigger picture—how her intimacy with Stu fit with her other men, especially Bob— could stay blurry. She could ignore it as too complex to break down into manageable bits. I don't believe I was being voyeuristic, but I was beginning to make headway in understanding my mother's moral world.

When the *Eridanus* returned to San Francisco on August 31, in the waiting mail Bob read musings from Ruth about joining the armed services. He responded by telegram and reiterated that "my opinion of the service is still the same"—he had opposed her enlisting—and reminded her that "once you're in, you're in. A person doesn't voluntarily resign in war time." He followed up with a letter reaffirming his opposition.

Two days later Ruth responded by telegram that she had received Bob's three telegrams and was "pleasantly surprised that you are back safely." She concluded her message by saying that she had "made no definite plans yet" and would "write you first." Then, for several weeks, silence.

Bob continued to write regularly. He routinely apologized for the "long time" if more than a day or two passed without writing. As Ruth's silence wore on, his frustration grew to the point that he "went out the other nite by myself and tried to take care of all the brandy in Frisco. All I can say, it was $17.00 wasted. And I'm very disgusted with myself because it was so blamed foolish." After more days passed and she still had sent no word, Bob pleaded: "Please dearest, I'm really begging now."

"In Bed with a Little Trouble"

Ruth may not have been current with her correspondence because she could not; she sent Bob a telegram telling him she was "in bed with a little trouble." "Dearest Invalid," he replied, "Don't know what you got, how you got it, but certainly hope you'll be on top in a few days—It would be to bad to come home on leave'n have you in your bunk, wouldn't it?" In a second letter on the same day, he wrote: "Hope your conscience bothers you enuf so you drop me a line. It seems as tho I've been back months + months and still I've heard from you only by telegram." He was "really in a blue mood" and added: "Please don't disappoint me."

"A little trouble" wasn't the only thing that had kept Ruth from writing. The September 23, 1943, edition of the *Two Rivers Reporter* noted that a "Miss Ruth L. Nelson, Minneapolis, arrived here this morning to take over her duties as the new public health nurse in this city."

How did Ruth land this job? Without a nursing degree she wouldn't have been qualified. Since these positions were likely filled by recent graduates of the University of Minnesota's nursing program, perhaps she had submitted an application before the end of the school year and Two Rivers never bothered to check whether she had earned her degree.

When Ruth finally broke her silence and wrote to Bob, she worried that her decision not to join the military might disappoint him. "Far from it," he replied. "I'm just plenty glad you missed the service." Ruth's worry struck me as odd, since Bob had repeatedly expressed his opposition to her joining the military. I doubted that her memory about such an important topic could be so short.

Perhaps she had confused Bob with another man who was gung-ho for the military. So many men, so little clarity.

The break in Ruth's letters had approached three weeks, a hiatus that followed Bob's months at sea, when they had been almost nonexistent. Now that Ruth had finally written in late September, I think he would have been justified in expecting an explanation. Instead Bob thanked her for writing, though he did admit that her failure to write for so long had left him "darn near crazy (with curiosity)."

Elsewhere his response indicates that she apologized for not writing sooner but offered no reason. In addition, Bob was wrestling with the uncertainties of Ruth's new situation and asked whether he still faced "the competition I had when you were in Wisconsin on that temporary duty." Presciently he added, "No fibbing." He had good reason to wonder whether she was telling the truth. Apparently she had written about one of the men but not the other.

Five days later Bob still pushed for resolution. "I know it's hard to remember subjects over a long period of time so am saving the letter you sent five days ago (the one it was so hard to write). Maybe you can tell me what you mean." Then he goaded: "But is there by any chance a third party is involved? Answer that one question and I'll know it all." What else could he think? The break in Ruth's letters had felt like an eternity to him. And when she was "in bed with a little trouble," she wouldn't say what the trouble was. Bob wouldn't have missed the double entendre of the phrase. To him her silent avoidance suggested competition.

Bob had to do what he could to hold his own. He knew that geographic distance worked against him, so he reiterated the hope that his fiancée would join him in California, an option that might look more attractive to her "after you've put in another winter wearing yourself out against the elements." He was encouraged that, since she hadn't signed a contract, she could get away quickly.

But Bob could do only so much. What Ruth might do continued to affect his decisions. When a fellow yeoman was leaving for officer training, Bob "was darn tempted to go back also but anticipated your being out here." Also, he still anticipated that she might "put up an argument" for delaying. He must have felt stuck.

"I Just Had an Idea I Could Fly"

Back in April 1942, when Bob had found himself in a similar rut, "getting impatient just sitting around waiting for something to happen," he had embarked on an adventure in decision making that anticipated what lay ahead for Ruth. It had started way back, as he wrote to Ruth: "I've ridden bikes, motorcycles, skooters, cars and trucks and I just had an idea I could fly too." A family story described his hope of joining the U.S. Army Air Corps when he enlisted, but his mother had put her foot down, insisting that it would be too dangerous. That did little to squelch his dream of flying.

First he asked several officers about his plan. All advised against it, so Bob decided to "just string along." Five months later, upon returning from the leave when he and Ruth got engaged, he wrote that he might "go to school + brush up on my math and then try and get in the Naval Air Corps," and asked Ruth to "let me know how you feel on the Air Corps issue."

Realizing at the outset that "it's hard to decide what to do," Bob applied himself to understand the differences between flying a plane and serving on a ship. He admitted that flying a plane had its dangers, "but they're losing loads and loads of men aboard ships now only nobody knows about it." Manning a gun on a ship required that you stay at your post. "No matter what they pour down on you all you can do is stay there and wait 'til they come back and you may be able to get a lucky shot in if a bomb don't get you and your gun's crew first." He elaborated: "See honey, when a bomb drops on a deck thousands of steel splinters fly just like a busted light bulb and some of those splinters are so small they can go inside you and leave no mark on the outside. They've already had a few cases where the guys complained of getting tired awfully quick so they took x-rays and found they had splinters lodged in their heart muscles. Course those guys were lucky cuz they were fixed up."

He figured that the probability for survival in the air was greater because "when you're in the air, you have the whole sky to move around in."

But then in the same letter Bob abruptly changed course, reflecting on "the effect flying will have on your body and heck it isn't worth it if you're going to be having trouble with your veins, brain, ears, eyes, or heart in later life. I'd rather be all there at 60 than be feeble minded, deaf, or have heart trouble." But he didn't stay with that thought long: "Course you do get excellent training in navigation, etc." And then he concluded: "I haven't really decided yet."

His indecision continued for months. Bob reported on advice he was receiving and that "about ten or twelve of the fellows are considering joining" the air corps. Old friend Pauly "is now in the army Air Corps and likes it swell," fellow Minnesotan John is "all hepped up about the Air Corps now," and fellow yeoman Dale has been "pushing me along for the Air Corps deal." Bob even planned "to see a kid who just washed out and see what it's like."

Then Bob wondered about the after-effects of the rapid change in air pressure on "heart, ears, and so forth" when "dive bombing and flying fighter planes." He asked Ruth whether she agreed that such effects were harmful, then said he figured "I'd rather take chances on the gun deck."

As Bob continued to waffle, his immediate supervisor, Wally, gave him "heck for even entertaining the thought of the Air Corps." In fact, "Wally said that my application would leave here but never get to Headquarters. Meaning he would dispose of it after it left the old man's office. Which he could very easily do." At this point Bob was prepared to stay where he was, as he wrote to Ruth: "It would be nice if I could stay here for a while, make chief, which Wally assured me was coming as soon as I had a year in, and then have you out here or near here."

Finally, in a January 1943 letter, Bob announced that "as far as the air service is concerned—it's out! Had a request all neatly made out and Wally said it was a foolish thing to do. It took him about 2 hours to get it off his chest." Reflecting on Wally's words and on his situation, Bob added: "Seeing I had such a good set up here with you coming out next summer and everything—Gee, when I stop and think of it I can hardly wait." Then to punctuate his point he imagined: "To be able to call up and talk with you and be able to bite your ear and give you hickeys."

But Bob changed course again. He passed the required physical examination and continued writing to Ruth about getting air corps training. In his effort to decide, he had asked officers for advice, discussed it for hours with his peers, and weighed the pros and cons in his own mind. He wrote to Ruth about it nineteen times, asking for her opinion six times. And still, a month later, he went "around and around again today" about the matter.

Bob's decision against the air corps probably came down to two factors: Wally's strongly worded advice and the realization that remaining in San Francisco would provide stability, increasing the likelihood of marrying Ruth. Whatever the reasons, he had finally made up his mind once and for all. He never wrote about the topic again.

Bob's convoluted decision making reflected wartime uncertainty. He didn't know what would happen next, where he might be sent, or what he might have to face at a moment's notice. A move by the enemy or decision by a superior could change everything, and he'd have to revisit his thinking all over again.

Meanwhile Ruth's decision making was similarly convoluted, as she continued to juggle the men in her life. She wrote a "nice long letter" to Stu, who replied that he "was glad to hear that you've gotten settled O.K. in Two Rivers." He hoped that "we could get together." Ruth's response was hardly reticent; he thanked her for her "grand letter." As before, the physical distance between them led him to "sure wish T. Rivers was closer." Then for the first time he ended a letter with Love. Stu was turning up the heat. Nor was he alone. A November letter from Ruth's mother, Lilly, advised her after a recent date: "Better go easy with that Doc—don't be too anxious."

The number of relationships Ruth maintained with other men in 1943 suggests that her commitment to Bob continued to wane. Even Werner sensed it: "You don't say much about Bob now. Be sure to be true to him or else break." None of the letters indicates that she took her father's advice.

"Aren't People Screwy?"

The war made it especially difficult to maintain romantic relationships as millions of people were moved all over the world. Lovers wanting to increase the odds that their relationship would survive often married more quickly than they would have in peacetime. By 1942 the marriage rate in the United States had soared to its highest level since 1920.[5]

Service personnel were well aware of the trend. "Did I ever tell you," Bob wrote, "about the girl who used to ride the bus with Fred every morning? She married a soldier after knowing him six days." And Russ wrote about what members of his squadron did during a recent leave: "One of the boys on our crew went up to

Kentucky with one of the other fellows + came back married. Our co-pilot, bombardier, and my asst. radio man all came back engaged. First thing you know, I'll be the only bachelor on the crew."

The war also stressed relationships by separating partners for long periods. And it ended relationships when people were killed. In response people altered their moral decision making. What had seemed right or wrong in peacetime changed during the war. A "schizoid morality" developed among service personnel—"one moral code for peace time in the home community and another for war time in a strange community."[6]

This schizoid morality could give lovers a reason to act bizarrely, as Bob knew:

> You'd a laughed yourself sick if you'd seen the fellow come down to muster this morning who was cut along both forearms and patches all over his head and face, and neck. He certainly was a sight. As you can imagine he got quite a razzing but it wasn't anything until the boys found out what it was for. He was rooming with a woman over town and last night her lawful husband came home. The kid didn't even stop for his pants. He showed up at the barracks in his shorts after traveling six blocks. From what he says the hubby didn't even lay a hand on him. He accounts for all the cuts and so forth from putting his hands over his face and jumping through the window. I'll bet the girl had some tall talking to do to her real man. Boy, oh boy, aren't people screwy?

Perhaps most distressing to many was the anxiety born of separation. Bob's continuous fretting had company: "Am listening to a song coming from the Supply Office—'I wonder who's kissing her now.' This same kid who's singing this song called his girl while we were in Seattle around 4 in the morning and started to apologize for awakening her and she said that she'd just come in herself—boy, he was really blue about that for a long time. Funny how something like that'll get a guy."

Bob tried to distance himself from the risk, as he wrote to Ruth about his office mate:

> His girl back in Iowa recently announced her engagement to an Army Officer and he, for a while, was a little bewildered thinking that it couldn't happen to him. Well, now here she comes back with a letter asking that he let bygones be bygones and that they kiss and make up. So he's writing her what a swell time he's having in California and that he isn't available. You know, honey, it's interesting to get in on someone else's love affairs. Especially, when you know yourself that you aren't going to be burnt.

But how could Bob be so sure? Could his certainty be nothing more than denial?

Denial it was. The incident that had ended his January 1943 visit to Minneapolis, when Bob had stumbled on that photograph of Ruth with another man, still rankled eight months later, which was "hard for me to admit especially when I raved about how anything like that would never bother me."

Bob's personal life remained as unsettled as ever. Professionally, though, he thrived. On October 14, 1943, he received word of his promotion to chief yeoman, effective September 16, "via the ship I had been stationed on last summer so it was a little late." The letters are silent about Ruth's sending congratulations. In contrast, when Russ was promoted to sergeant, Ruth promptly congratulated him.

Bob's time aboard the USS *Eridanus* had fulfilled a prerequisite for officer training. But now as chief yeoman, a noncommissioned officer, his perspective changed. When Ruth asked whether he would continue pursuing officer training, he replied that he would "rather stay right where I am" and explained that "I'd rather be Chief and a regular guy than be an officer and so full of hot air I'd almost blow up."

"Meeting in Chicago Is Just Plenty Okay"

Now, for only the second time in all the letters, Ruth proposed that she and Bob meet. This time she suggested Chicago, an idea Bob greeted enthusiastically: "Meeting in Chicago is just plenty okay." But when she wrote that they should have separate rooms, he saw the idea as "a little silly" and added: "You know as well as I do that I won't be in my room or vice versa so we'll get our room together." In responding to her desire to keep the trip a secret, he reassured her that he hadn't said anything about it to anyone else.

I saw that secrecy as Ruth's way of justifying the tryst. She could feel confident that she wasn't sinning so long as it wouldn't become known. At first I considered this another example of the careful parsing that, I increasingly realized, characterized her morality. Meeting her fiancé would be good; sharing a room would be bad. The longer I lived with this new reality, though, the more I came to understand that, for Ruth, morality had most to do with her public image. If she could keep others from discovering her morally questionable actions, then she could affirm her sense of righteousness. The unblemished public image would bolster her wandering self, affirming that she was somehow okay.

To accomplish the meeting, Bob arranged to transport a prisoner from San Francisco to New York. While on the "really rugged" trip east, the pair stopped to visit Bob's uncle Carl and his family. The letters are mum about this; I learned of it in a phone conversation with Bob's cousin Ruth. When Bob arrived, she said, he announced that he had a girlfriend to whom he had given their address and asked if any mail had come.

Uncle Carl retrieved a letter and gave it to Bob. "You should've seen the look on his face when he saw that letter!" Cousin Ruth exclaimed, and I felt that moment come alive. She had given me an eyewitness account of my father's radiant delight, something I had never seen myself.

Cousin Ruth and Bob had a special bond because they shared a birthday, though twelve years apart. He offered to take her to the local five-and-dime, and the twelve-year-old felt like a grownup as she walked along the street with Bob, who was all decked out in his dress blue uniform. At the store he urged her to pick out whatever she wanted. She chose a baton and he responded, "That's all? Why don't you get some candy too?" When they went to check out, the young woman behind the counter tried her best to get Bob's attention. He didn't miss a beat: "Better luck next time, honey. I'm already taken."

Bob had written to Ruth that, on his way back from delivering the prisoner to New York, he would be staying at the Fort Dearborn Hotel in Chicago from November 5 to 8. "If we miss making connections in Chicago we'll miss each other all together. Gee, hon, don't fail me." Ruth didn't fail Bob, at least in the sense that she showed up and spent these few days with him.

Bob wrote his next letter on his way back and mailed it in Denver on November 11. Many of the hundreds of letters in Ruth's box are written in Bob's hasty cursive. Many others he typed single-spaced without margins, cramming as much as he could on each page. Still others he scrawled on scraps of paper or the backs of envelopes. Bob filled all these letters with unguarded feelings and unfiltered thoughts, a stream of consciousness flowing onto the page.

But the one he wrote now was entirely different. He printed every word in careful capital letters with wide spacing between lines. Not one word appears to be spontaneous. Each gives the impression of thoughtful intention and comes laden with pain:

DEAR BABE:

TO BAD WE COULDN'T MAKE THIS A COUPLE TRIP BUT SINCE, WELL, IT'S TO BAD.

SAY HONEY, I'VE FINALLY COME TO THE CONCLUSION THAT YOU AND I ARE GOING TO BUST. I REALIZE NOW, HONEY, WHEN I STOP AND THINK OF ALL THE ARGUMENTS YOU OFFERED THAT YOU APPARENTLY AREN'T IN LOVE WITH ME. YOU UNDERSTAND WHAT I MEAN, DON'T YOU, HON? I'M HOPING IT MAY TURN OUT THAT YOU'RE IN LOVE BUT AS YET AREN'T AWARE OF IT. SINCE WE AGREE IN EVERYTHING AND HAVE ALL THE MUTUAL RESPECT FOR ONE ANOTHER THAT WE NEED I'M HOLDING THE HOPE THAT THIS'S THE CASE.

WOULD APPRECIATE IF YOU'D SEND THE BANK BOOK TO ME ALTHO I STILL INTEND TO LEAVE THE ACCOUNT JOINT. (STILL HOPIN') THE RING, AS LONG AS YOU DON'T WEAR IT, MAY AS WELL BE IN FRISCO. YOU SEEM TO HAVE SOMETHING "IN THE FIRE" SO WE MAY AS WELL MAKE IT A QUICK , CLEAN BREAK . -(-AND A HARD ONE TOO -)-

BE A GOOD GIRL — SNOOKS — LET ME HEAR FROM YOU — CAN WE KEEP IT BETWEEN OURSELVES? PLEASE.

LOVINGLY yOURS
Bob

PS (LONGINGLY TOO)

What happened in Chicago? Bob's anticipation of their meeting couldn't have been higher, but this letter couldn't be lower. For two years now he had been very public about his love for "Ruthie." His parents approved, and he had made clear to his service mates that he was committed to her. No longer. Nothing remained now but pain. His *PLEASE* was a whimper.

Returning to San Francisco gave Bob second thoughts. "First I write a letter 'reading' you off," he began, "then I'm sorry for it so now I don't know how I stand." Not only was he unclear where he stood with her, he struggled "to shake you but my mind just can't seem to think with out thinking of you. In some way or other you've always been behind what ever I've done so you can see it's a little difficult. Somehow honey," he concluded, "it seems that I'm suffering (by not having you in Cal.) for some one else's mistake so please don't be to firm in your conviction that Two Rivers is your only consolation."

"No, They Don't Know About Yours!"

Bob's next letter returned to the old pattern of his feeling down while "patiently awaiting" a letter from Ruth. The old pattern, though, brought a new agitation, apparently since the time in Chicago, as revealed in the contrasting images in the closing. He signed off with "a little sigh"—perhaps wondering what might have been—and "a great big tentative kiss"—still hoping for what yet might be. His postscript explains. Writing about his immediate supervisor, he reported: "For your information, Donna, Wally's wife, just got [illegible] around a month ago and No, They don't know about [illegible]!"

Again Ruth had scribbled out words, so I figured that I had stumbled upon another sensitive subject. What had Donna gotten? Fired? Pregnant? An illness? And I hadn't a clue what Wally and Donna didn't know about.

In an effort to get the letter to reveal its secret, I turned it over and examined it carefully. Nothing. I held it up to the light streaming through the window into my office. Still nothing. Efforts with a slide projector and other lamps were equally unavailing. When I realized that I wouldn't be able to crack it on my own, I visited a company that specializes in restoring historical works. Still no go. The staff there suggested that I try putting the letter under different colors of light, either physically, by trying colored theatrical gels on a bulb, or by scanning the passage into a computer and using photographic software. A photographer friend took on the challenge. She spent an hour or more trying different colors, and then, as if yielding to a magic formula, the sentence emerged crystal clear: "Donna, Wally's wife, just got an abortion around a month ago and No, They don't know about yours!"

An abortion! And, Ruth told Bob, the father was Greg. No wonder their meeting in Chicago ended in disaster.

Ruth's unwanted pregnancy must have been devastating. It would present stark alternatives: on the one hand, carrying a life-shattering baby to term with all the terrifying unknowns implicit in that decision; on the other hand, terminating this potential new life. Stark, indeed agonizing.

Some of those terrifying prospects were clear. For example, in the 1940s the belief that a woman shouldn't be both worker and mother was widespread, and the City of Two Rivers would not likely keep an unwed mother on as city nurse. Other unknowns presented question marks: How would her parents react? Or Greg? Would Bob—or anyone—still want her, pregnant with someone else's child? But the biggest problem of all was existential: Could she be a mother at all, especially without a husband? What should or could she do now?

Because of Ruth's background, there would be additional agony. In the subculture of Swedish American Baptists in those days, people who committed sexual sins were especially scorned. Sin if you must, but don't engage in illicit sex, or you will, like Hester Prynne, bear the mark of shame. An out-of-wedlock baby would have personified that shame. Ruth might have seen abortion as the lesser evil. So long as it could be kept secret, perhaps she could preserve her image as a faithful, untainted Christian.

As troubled as I had been by the revelations of Ruth's dating life and academic failure, nothing could have prepared me for the shock of her out-of-wedlock pregnancy and its termination. I, too, had been raised in my mother's version of the Swedish American Baptist subculture; I, too, found sexual activity beyond its strictures difficult to accept. As my own faith has evolved I have, I hope, let go of its judgmental aspects. But when my mother was involved, old reactions died hard.

And when the letters revealed such incendiary material, I also had to choose whether to include it in this narrative. At first I retreated, embarrassed and ashamed. By omitting this part of the story, I could have kept Ruth's secrets. I could have retained the preletters version of my mother, the version I wanted to believe in. I wouldn't have had to make the painful changes to family lore about my mother.

But I had reached the point of no return. To maintain my previously unexamined understanding of my mother, I would have had to deny what I was learning. Since I couldn't bring myself to do that, I decided that everything belonged in the story. The whole truth needed to be known—the good, the bad, and the ugly. Continuing the old version of family lore would have denied the whole truth.

Learning and affirming the whole truth was profoundly liberating. Before, when all I had to go on was what family lore had taught me, my understanding of Ruth was more ideal than real: the sterling student and preacher's kid who had always lived a pious example of Christian faith. Now, as I learned of her premarital pregnancy and abortion, she was brought down to Earth: a more fully human, more fully lifelike woman who struggled with predicaments like those that afflict us all. I am saddened that I did not experience her this way while she was alive.

Yet I understand why my mother refrained from telling me. She would have felt too ashamed. She wouldn't have wanted to disgrace Bob. And she might have even considered it irrelevant to me—why would I need to know? In the end, though, the letters told me posthumously. I believe she actually hoped they would.

I feel deep compassion for the desperate woman Ruth had become. I later learned that her abortion, though illegal, had been performed as safely as possible—her friend Veronica serving as nurse, Veronica's friend John as doctor—and I also feel gratitude that Ruth avoided the dangers of infection, sterility, or death that commonly attended back-alley procedures. I have renewed appreciation for the legality of abortion today.

Since Bob and Ruth didn't write about what happened in Chicago, I can only speculate. Ruth wouldn't have wanted to report the abortion by letter, so she hadn't written to Bob about it. Neither would she have wanted to jeopardize their time together by telling him at the beginning. So she likely waited to tell him until shortly before they parted. She would have recalled the "little trouble" from the previous September that had kept her in bed for a few days, and he would have remembered her reticence to provide details. For him the news about the abortion would have clarified those mysterious letters but with devastating emotional impact.

The havoc of the operation was traumatic enough, especially for a woman from Ruth's religious background, but the fear of prosecution made it even worse. Abortion wasn't uncommon—a nationally recognized authority estimated that at least 681,000 abortions were performed annually during the 1930s in the United States—but performing one was illegal.[7] By the time of Ruth's abortion, some states, including Minnesota, had begun aggressively prosecuting doctors who offered abortions. Their patients were often forced to testify, on pain of a contempt citation or even jail. When a woman who had an abortion refused to testify at a 1949 abortion trial in Chicago, for example, the judge cited her for contempt of court and ordered her to jail for six months. One night in jail convinced the woman to testify the next day.

In criminal abortion trials patients had to speak publicly of pregnancy and abortion in front of a predominantly male audience of judge, attorneys, officials, and newspaper reporters. If the women had been unmarried, they had to admit in court the illicit exercise of their sexuality and sometimes name their lovers. Ruth faced a frightening situation.[8]

Her pregnancy and the potential legal troubles following the abortion would have been disturbing enough for Bob. But that the man responsible was Greg—the family friend and landlady's son—aggravated Bob even more. More than two months later his anger still simmered: "I can't understand what ever possessed you to go with him in the first place. He just doesn't seem to be your type." At the same time Bob might even have felt some secret relief, the abortion a sign that Ruth wasn't committed to Greg. Bob could see the possibility of redemption, urging that Ruth should "never forget the lesson" to stop "playing around" and remain faithful to him alone.

Though he may not have considered what he wrote to Ruth in his next letter as an example of "the lesson," I find it hard to believe otherwise as he wrote about a liberty on Thanksgiving night:

There was one blonde (Norski) in a place last night who was doing all right by herself. That is to say she was doing her drinking and holding a conversation with everyone but wasn't obligating herself to any one man. They started closing up the place (12 o'clock) and as I was just across from her I could hear at least nine or ten men offer to take her home, or take her out to eat a bite before she turned in. Some of them had one line and some had others. And baby, some of those lines were original. Of course, I left before she did but on my way down to the cable car I bumped into her again cutting across a parking lot. I was really surprised to see her alone. She crossed and went into her place. That's the first girl I've ever seen who wasn't to be fooled or foiled by vanity. She had her bf in the Navy. But she certainly went thru a lot of temptation. She [was] my inspiration, not for the gal that she was, just for the model she was.

I wondered how Ruth felt when she read that. Would she have seen it as Bob imagined—as an inspirational story—or would she have felt guilty for not having resisted such temptation? Or perhaps she felt it as a reproof for having been "fooled or foiled by vanity" herself.

As the weeks passed, Bob slowly returned to his former pattern of writing. Though he still signed his letters with the cooler *Bob*, he described himself "laying quietly and thinking of you, I can almost realize you being alongside of me." He attributed this renewed sense of intimacy to "our last time together" but added it would eventually "do us both more harm than good the longer we stay apart." He wanted to persuade Ruth that something had to change soon if they were to have a future together. But past experience left him "thinking of all this time we've wasted and getting 'bluer' by the minute."

What Bob wanted to see change was Ruth's location: "I think there's enough in the bank so you could come out here and loaf around for a while before you decided on something." Yet he admitted that he "didn't hold much hope for your getting away." Stumbling on some condoms didn't help: "Was cleaning out my locker this evening and found the 'raincoats' which were left over since our time together. Then I really got lonesome."

And Bob saw an even worse consequence of their geographic separation: "If you can't [come] then I'm starting to move, and we may as well then, call it pretty well off." The thought of this made him feel down since he didn't see any other attractive options: "Don't want to start chasing around cause some times fate can play some serious tricks as you well know—huh? So much for memories."

"Be Careful of Those Petting Officers!"

Shortly before Ruth had met Bob in Chicago, she had gone out with Mike, a doctor and lieutenant in the navy who was probably stationed at the Coast Guard station in Two Rivers. On their date Mike had reported that he was soon to ship out to San Diego. Ruth would have responded that her brother and sister-in-law lived in San Diego and that she had thought of moving west someday. Mike wrote to update her on his plans and included this offer: "If you have decided to seek your fortune out yonder I should be more than happy to help you by giving you transportation on my burro! Let me know if you decide in that fashion."

Reporting Mike's invitation wasn't the best choice of topics for Ruth's first letter to Bob since the disastrous time in Chicago. Nevertheless she asked him what he thought about it. He warned her that "any doc in the service of Uncle Sam can be, or should be, pretty virile." Whatever she decided, he urged her to "be sure and let me know so I can do all I can for arrangements etc." The six hundred miles between San Diego and San Francisco may have suited Ruth's feeling of uncertainty about Bob—closer but not too close. For him the distance would have been frustrating—closer but not close enough.

Ruth scribbled at the bottom of Bob's letter: "Didn't go with Doc. Good thing, I guess." When did she write that—when Mike left for San Diego? Or perhaps days, months, or years later when, upon rereading it, she reflected on what might have been? Whenever she wrote it, she hesitated about how good her decision was, adding that wistful "I guess."

Meanwhile, despite all Bob's hopes and admonitions, Ruth continued to date and correspond with the other men. She wrote a letter, Christmas card, and note to her former classmate Lee, who responded with "a real long" letter. As for Russ, after he had shipped out to England, he reflected: "It sure was good to see you again when I was home. By the way, am I still correct in writing Miss? I didn't know, as you said when I was home that 'Bob' was expecting a furlough soon. Whatever you do, you know you have my best wishes."

Ruth also continued writing to Stu. In his second letter of November, he probed: "How's your love life coming along outside of your navy deal? I suppose you've charmed the local lads that are left by now!" Those lads might have been those working in a munitions factory nearby and staying in a boardinghouse across the street from Ruth's place—now the home of the Two Rivers Historical Society. The local Coast Guard station also prompted to warn: "But be careful of those Petting Officers!" On the envelope, Ruth wrote: "Answered 12/11/43." Stu clearly didn't see her "navy deal" as a hindrance to socializing, nor did she appear to discourage him. Responding to her "much belated letter" later in December, he asked whether she was "coming to the wild party New Years Eve at Eddies—bring a jug of wine! Also a camera!"

Stu's first letter of 1944 asked if Ruth had heard from Veronica lately. He had learned "from one of her friends that she plans on being married in June!" Two weeks later Ruth wrote back, and Stu replied that he had received her "nice letter this week" upon returning home after a business trip. Then he asked: "When do you expect to visit us back here in Mpls? Nancy says she has a place for you and you always can use the bunk room at [my house]! Since my brother has moved I have the other twin bed open too!"

I want to believe that Stu's invitation to share "the other twin bed" in his room—an aggressive form of flirtation symptomatic of those crazy war years—reflected more on him than on Ruth. Yet Stu's invitation to attend a party with alcohol didn't square with the mother I knew. She wasn't a drinker, not even wine with a meal. There was no alcohol in the household, and the one and only drink I ever saw her imbibe was the martini with which she celebrated my doctoral degree. So Stu's mentioning wine surprised me. Nothing in the letters refers to friends teasing her about abstinence or applying pressure on her to drink. To the contrary, as Stu does here, her friends appear to have taken for granted that she would join them. For her this would have represented a flagrant departure from her faith, an activity that her parents would have seen as backsliding and decadent.

My mother raised me to believe that committed Christians don't drink, a belief I practiced from childhood through my college years. The first challenge to this belief occurred while I was on tour with a school chorus after my first year at Bethel College, a school founded by Swedish Baptists whose lifestyle expectations required abstinence from alcohol. At a Baptist church in Sweden, supper included beer! How ironic, I thought: a congregation in the Swedish Baptist tradition was serving us an alcoholic beverage.

Later, when I was in seminary, I actually gave the matter some thought. If drinking is to be forbidden, I remember asking, then why does John's Gospel report that Jesus turned water to wine at a wedding? Not only that, the chief steward marveled: "Everyone serves the good wine first, and then the inferior wine after the guests have become drunk. But you have kept the good wine until now" (John 2:10). And what about such texts as "there is nothing outside a person that by going in can defile, but the things that come out are what defile" (Mark 7:15)? I came to see alcohol as part of God's good creation and abstinence as the kind of empty legalism that Jesus condemned. So I began to drink occasionally. I also abandoned some of the other lifestyle rules that seemed to smack of gnostic dualism: I danced, went to movies, played weekend games of whist till 2 A.M.

Stu's letter took me back to that time in my life. Though I had difficulty imagining my mother attending a wild party, her change in lifestyle, albeit temporary, resonated with me. Had we ever compared notes about our young adult years in this respect, we would have found common ground. But by the time I was on the scene, she had returned to her teetotaling way.

This period of Ruth's life never made it into family lore. On one hand, I can understand why wild parties, deception, promiscuity, an out-of-wedlock pregnancy, and an illegal abortion are not the kinds of memories a parent readily shares with children. On the other hand, selectively sharing bits of them at appropriate times might have helped me to feel closer to my mother, especially as I began to move away from the version of faith that we had shared.

•

Shortly after 1944 began, Bob's uncertainty about Ruth intensified. As usual he hadn't received a letter from her for some time, leading him to begin his first letter of the new year: "Was going to try and outlast you by our silence in letter writing but your letter received today changed everything." But that letter didn't keep him from asking, "What or who's been taking up your time?"

Ruth's letter, the one that "changed everything," raised issues beyond fidelity. I can infer from Bob's response what she may have written:

Then, Now

Ruth: *I'm concerned that if the abortion is discovered, it could land me in jail. To be on the safe side, maybe I should drop out of sight for a while. Are you with me on this?*

Bob: Yes shortie, I'm with you. I don't think it'll mean jail or even a loss of reputation. So please don't worry or get to upset about it. And your disappearing wouldn't help. But if circumstances press you to much back there (2 Rivers) you're certainly welcome to come out here.

Then he caught himself: "WAIT A MINUTE, that is with the understanding that you've learned your lesson and are definitely not playing around." With his anger rekindled he thundered: "I'm telling you now kiddo, as much as I love you, if you ever raise even the slightest suspicion of straying you and I are through, and Baby, that goes even as good friends." Even so, he ended his letter, "I'm with you—100%."

Though Ruth seemed to have repented, Bob was far from convinced that she could keep herself from straying again. Having apparently kept to the moral high ground—or at least tried to convince her that he had—he was now demanding that she join him there. Could she? Would she?

Broken trust was Ruth's biggest hurdle. With the relationship itself in doubt, Bob would submit every future promise in every letter to special scrutiny, trying to discern whether Ruth meant what she said. She would have to convince a skeptical Bob that she would remain faithful only to him. At this point I could see that rebuilding trust would be difficult. With their communication only through letters, this would also take time, if it could be done at all. Even though I knew that my parents eventually married, I felt myself wondering, over and over, how their relationship could survive.

By the end of January Bob had returned to opening his letters with "Dear Bunnie" and to signing them with "Bobbie." His affection was warming but not easily. He received Ruth's next letter as "without reservation, one of the most discouraging letters I've ever received from you. There's even discouragement in reading between the lines. Not that I'm meaning to say anything against the letter, No, no, but what you were trying to put across was anything but good." As a result he "could really tell you a few things," but, uncertain how she might take them, he would "skip it 'til we meet again." Trusting Ruth with his deeper thoughts and feelings would have to wait.

The next few lines of Bob's letter showed me that something besides Ruth's relationship with Greg kept trust at bay. When Ruth wrote that she couldn't understand why Bob wanted to leave San Francisco, he replied: "Honestly, hon, in all the time I've been out here I've seen nothing but filth and corruption and I'm sick and tired of it. Everyone going out with everyone else's wife when either one or the other feels like it. I'm beginning to doubt if there is such a thing as loyalty left." Given the context, I don't think Bob aimed that last sentence at Ruth. But I wondered how it may have hit her. Did she see it through his eyes, the result of a decadent situation only he had to live with? Or did she imagine herself as one of the "everyone going out," causing her to become wracked with guilt? Whatever the case, he could still sign off with "I love you and mean it more than ever."

On February 18 Bob penned a passing comment: "Certainly good news on Truk, isn't it?" For the previous forty-eight hours U.S. aircraft had bombed Truk (now known as Chuuk) to destroy this headquarters of the Japanese Imperial Navy. He couldn't have foreseen that a son of his would conduct anthropological research in that group of islands in Micronesia. Now I felt a new connection to him as he named a place that had come to mean so much to me.

But beyond a few history buffs, scuba divers, or Pacific anthropologists, who in my generation had ever heard of Chuuk? When I told friends where I did anthropological fieldwork, I was usually met with blank stares. Not so my father, I now realized, though he never talked about Chuuk with me. I also realized how different his mental picture of Chuuk must have been. I knew it as a place for research; he knew it as a war zone.

"Yes, It's Trouble All Right"

Throughout this period Ruth had worries that went far beyond the question of fidelity. Though the letters are not completely explicit, a combination of reading between the lines and later correspondence suggests the following:

> Ruth's abortion had been performed in Minneapolis by John, the doctor who had been engaged to Ruth's nursing school friend Veronica. In November 1943 Veronica broke up with John and, by the end of that year, became engaged to Randall. When John heard the news, he decided to make one last try to get Veronica back. He asked her to break off her engagement to Randall and marry him instead. When she refused, he resorted to blackmail, threatening to inform the authorities about the abortion that he had performed on Ruth—a threat that implicated his own career and Ruth's, of course, but also Veronica's because she had assisted in the procedure. Veronica remained steadfast in her refusal.

Bob wrote that John's threat was "probably a bluff," but since everyone involved is "so concerned about reputations, etc., it may be his only solution." In another letter he wrote the same day, Bob said he had reported "the whole story" to Wally, his immediate supervisor, who is "under the opinion that if anything comes of it that you should immediately resign and come out here." Two weeks later Bob goaded: "I can't figure out why in the heck you 'horse' around back there. All it takes is one word from [John]. So why the hell don't you clear out." Wally again chimed in that Ruth should "get your tail out here before you're quietly held for investigation."

So often did Bob go to Wally and Donna's house that they and their two young boys had become a surrogate family, a home away from home. These days, whenever he visited, he talked about the situation ensnaring Ruth. He forwarded their advice: "They think it would be worth it to Veronica to marry [John] just to save all reputations concerned. This way Veronica's the only one who's hurt and then the possibility is she may enjoy it but otherwise 3 people are hurt—See?"

Ruth must have written to Bob that she assumed John would let her know in advance when he was going to speak to the authorities. If so, she figured, she could leave Two Rivers before the authorities could find her. Bob disagreed, arguing that "if he's smart he's not going to tell you all about it first—Because you're the main subject." After underscoring that advice in red, he made his pitch again: "The longer you can stall for time the harder it'll be for them to prove anything—And the best place to stall for time's out here."

Ruth wanted to stall for time all right but not in California. Instead she planned to visit, of all places, Minneapolis. Her not telling Bob why she wanted to go there fed his suspicion that Greg was involved—he came home from the army whenever he had leave—so Bob admonished her to "stay away from Greg's place particularly." By the time Bob wrote his next letter, though, he conceded that he couldn't prevent her from going and wrote off her proposed trip as "your business."

Bob's dismay was aggravated by what happened next. When he received two "wonderful letters" from Ruth in the same brown envelope, he must have been thrilled. But then he noticed the rank she had written after his name: Y1c. He hadn't been a yeoman first class since September 1943, when he had made the leap to chief petty officer. As with all military personnel, Bob's rank comprised a significant part of his identity. For Ruth to use his previous rank—four months out of date—must have seemed incomprehensible. At first he waved aside her blunder—"you must've been dreaming"—but by end of the paragraph the hurt led him to offer a sarcastic forgiveness. I wondered if she understood.

Ruth's confusion about Bob's rank only added to his continuing anxiety about Greg. In Bob's next letter he wrote that, if she had not heard news of Greg lately, "you undoubtedly will in Mpls." As much as Bob hoped otherwise, a meeting between the two seemed inevitable. Why else, Bob might have wondered, would she risk being served with a subpoena? Being summoned to testify before a grand jury? Maybe even sent to jail? This may have been what haunted Bob when he wrote that her affair with Greg "seems to be bothering me more now than it did [last November when you told me about it]." Still aggrieved, Bob would have doubted more than ever how much he could count on Ruth. The most he could venture was "you seem pretty certain you love me."

The trouble building in Minneapolis didn't involve Greg, though, but came crashing down from a different direction. While finishing a lengthy reply to Ruth's most recent letter, Stu heard breaking news on KSTP, the Twin Cities radio station, about Veronica and Ruth being "all mixed up in a affair with a Dr. John Schmidt! Boy! What a sorrid affair! Just what was it all about? Another one of Veronicas double crossing deals with her lovers? I'm surprised you got mixed up in it. I thought you'd had enough of her deals!"

Perhaps Veronica had called Ruth to plead with her to help fend off John's last-ditch advances. But after Ruth arrived in Minneapolis, something went terribly wrong, and Ruth ended up as part of a news story.

The next day Stu added another postscript before mailing the letter: "You sure must have made a rush trip. I called Veronica's to talk to you + you'd already gone back to Two Rivers. I wondered why you had'nt even called me or Nancy? Well, I'll wait to hear your story. Hope you were'nt hurt in the deal."

Stu's elliptical commentary tantalized me. What could have happened? What was so sordid and sufficiently scandalous to have been reported on the radio? The letters remained frustratingly opaque, and I found some clarification only on microfilm from the Minnesota Historical Society. On January 31, 1944, the date of Stu's postscript, the *Minneapolis Star Journal* ran this story on its front page: "Possible Grand Jury Action Seen in Case of Doctor Injured in Car After Quarrel." Dr. John Schmidt, the paper reported, had rolled his car twice and had been hospitalized in a coma and listed in critical condition. According to police, the accident had followed an argument between the doctor and his former fiancée.

[Police] said the girl told them Dr. Schmidt drove her to Bloomington township . . . and there pulled a revolver. He told her, she said, that he had nothing left to live for, and was going to "take her with him."

She said she finally persuaded him to give her the gun, and she fired two shots into the ground to empty it, then clicked the trigger repeatedly and believed it empty.

She learned later the gun still had three cartridges in the cylinder, but that they were nicked and failed to fire.

Then, she said, he took a hypodermic needle from the glove compartment and attempted to jab it into her leg. She broke the needle, however.

Then, she said, he attempted to choke her, and, outside the car, she broke away from him three times and three times was dragged back to the car.

During the struggle, she said, he broke his glasses. Able to see only poorly without them, he asked her to drive the car.

She drove, she said, until she came to a farmhouse, and there jammed on the brakes and jumped from the car. She ran to the farmhouse, she said, screaming for help.

The farmhouse was abandoned, and she hid there till the doctor drove away, then ran some distance to another farmhouse, where she used the telephone to call police. In the interim Schmidt rolled his car.

Veronica's account to police reminded me of a bad movie. But its plot turns were so bizarre that maybe her story was true although hard to believe. And the newspaper didn't mention Ruth. I wondered about her involvement—which was enough to have been mentioned in the radio broadcast but not the newspaper story. Since the letters are silent on this point, I am left with my own speculation:

Upon receiving a telephone call for help from a distressed Veronica, Ruth left for Minneapolis and arrived at Veronica's place. Sometime later John drove up and demanded that Veronica go with him, alone. Hoping to talk some sense into him, she agreed and they drove away. Hours passed. Then Veronica called. She was at the police station and asked Ruth to come. Veronica was telling Ruth what had happened when the KSTP reporter found them and included Ruth's name in the breaking news story. Terrified that such public exposure might get her arrested because of the abortion, Ruth fled before the newspaper reporter arrived and before she could call Stu.

Veronica and Randall abandoned their June wedding date. Instead they wed immediately, with the next day's newspaper listing the bare fact of their marriage in its small-font summary of legal transactions. When Bob learned of it, he asked, "Do you think Veronica's knot'll last?"

Three days later the same newspaper reported that John Schmidt had died. The coroner announced that he had opened an investigation after learning that Schmidt was being treated for "phenobarbital poisoning" at the time of his death.

Presumably Ruth and Veronica could relax momentarily as the illegal abortion hadn't become public. Still, they had plenty to worry about, including a coroner nosing around for evidence that could implicate either of them in illegal activity.

In response to Ruth's letter about John's desperate descent, Stu advised, "As you say, the only thing to do now is to forget the whole unfortunate incident and remember the lesson it teaches." No one elaborated on what the lesson was. Was it never to become too passionate? Or knowing when to take no for an answer? Or did it have something to do with overdosing on a drug? What lesson did John's death have to teach? Perhaps everyone knew, so it didn't have to be mentioned. Or perhaps no one knew, so a platitude sufficed.

If the lesson was obscure, others in Ruth's life didn't hesitate to suggest how the tragedy might have been averted. Lilly—who wouldn't have known about the abortion—wrote that "maybe John wouldn't be dead now if you had lived so close to Christ that you could have shown him the right way—didn't he sort of turn to you." Whether Lilly's speculation filled Ruth with guilt or rolled off her back as a motherly nag is impossible to know.

And Bob added his guilt-laden surmise: "Of course, I can always say that if you'd been out here it would perhaps've never happened." The tragedy suggested to him that "there's one person left who's liable to get murdered yet and I believe you know who that is. Yes, little Greggie." In the same letter Bob wrote that the "John and Veronica case" had made him "much more disgusted and restless." Bob was not privy to the recent coverage in the Minneapolis news media, so he expressed worry about family members who "may still be plenty shocked if a grand jury investigation comes up."

Given the physical distance between them and the gnawing uncertainty of Ruth's legal situation, Bob renewed his suggestion that she join him in California. This time he tried to make his suggestion more enticing by adding that it "would be much easier if we were married." Bringing up marriage, though, reminded him of his frustration: "If you want to get married, F-I-N-E—but if you're going to chase around for a while then chase around. Truthfully, I'm tired of our indecision."

In his next letter Bob addressed a source of Ruth's resistance: "You seem to have the idea that you can't work after you get married. What would you do just sitting around an apartment all day long? You'd go nuts!" Having "written like this many times before" and acknowledging "it gets tiresome to read letters along this line," he concluded: "If you're coming out I'm sticking around and taking school. But, if you're not, then I'm moving."

While Bob tried to lay down an ultimatum, Ruth remained mum. "You said in your last letter," he wrote, "you were going to tell me all about the latest happenings and your latest decisions. But as yet I'm still in the dark."

"Does Brother Kowalski Still Stand a Chance?"

While Bob struggled Russ soared. Two months had passed since Russ had last written, in part because he wondered if "ole' man Russ had been taken off your mailing list completely!" On February 16 Russ wrote of his relief when he "received your X'mas card & letter of Dec. 22, today! And I assure you it was bothering me a great deal too, so you can see I was very glad to hear from you today!"

Later in the letter Russ, who was still in England and unaware of the news reports in Minneapolis, noted that Veronica is "deserting us and getting married. I hope you'll get time off to be there for the big occasion as I have very high hopes of making it myself!"

Then he dropped a bomb: "Maybe we should make it a double occasion! You think I'm just kidding don't you? Incidentally, what is the status of your left hand these days? Does brother Kowalski still stand a chance?"

Never before had Russ written so forcefully. I wondered how Ruth would respond. Would she be excited and drawn to him? Or would she be afraid and pull back? Or, with so much already weighing on her, would she simply freeze, confused about what to do?

Two days later Russ waxed nostalgic: "I still have your photograph with me. Wouldn't mind being where I was the night I got it. Remember?" This memory triggered another: "Did you ever mention anything to Veronica about our being in the Hasty-Tasty that night? I've often wondered if she knew it!" Then he pushed: "If you got the letter I wrote a couple days ago, read it over again and think over the little suggestion I made, huh? Maybe you think I'm crazy, but I assure you, my sweet, I'm still in my right mind."

"There Seems to Be Something Occupying Your Mind Right Now"

On February 28 Bob traveled 230 miles south to Morro Bay and reported for beach patrol duty. The Coast Guard's beach patrol, primarily a security force, was charged with detecting and monitoring activities of enemy vessels offshore. Family lore had it that my father had been stationed at Morro Bay and patrolled the coast on horseback.

I had visited Morro Bay before I knew of the letters. Even today it's a stark place. A huge rock offshore looms over the entrance to the harbor while sand eddies whirl in the wind. My wife and I bundled up against the June chill for the short walk to the Morro Bay State Park Museum of Natural History. While an elderly docent shared his youthful memories of the beach patrol, I tried to imagine my father riding along the beach while scanning the horizon for signs of the enemy. That was hard because nothing much remains from the war years. No trace of stables, and the navy base is long gone, demolished shortly after the war to make way for a power plant.

Bob's move to Morro Bay must have provided more culture shock. He had left the intensity of San Francisco in its role as Gateway to the Pacific, and his new challenge meant adapting to a small base in a hamlet of only four hundred people. On one hand, I couldn't see how this desolate and barren place could have helped him overcome his persistent loneliness and anxiety. On the other hand, he was never one for crowds. And he enjoyed being around horses—as a boy he sometimes helped his father deliver milk with a horse-drawn wagon. Perhaps the rugged terrain, salt air, and rolling surf would provide just the tonic he needed.

Or perhaps not. He had barely gotten his bag unpacked in Morro Bay before the anxious worry returned. He sensed from Ruth's last letter that "there seems to be something occupying your mind right now." Then he speculated what that might be: "Has Greg been home on furlough? You mentioned he never did get overseas."

I could find no evidence that Ruth disabused Bob of his hunch. If so, I doubted that his new assignment would bring him any assurance about Ruth. After all, his move there confirmed, at least in his mind, that she would not be joining him anytime soon.

"Where Are All Your Promises?"

Ruth was also contending with her parents' becoming "more and more grieved" by what they read in her letters. They had lent her hundreds of dollars over the years for school, a considerable sum in Depression-era America. Though she was now working a full-time job, she had yet to begin repaying them. Far from feeling apologetic about neglecting her debt, she wrote: "I am glad if I can pay my keep and have both my Hospitalization and other insurance paid up and save a little besides. At the end of a year, Daddy, you'll say that I have been pretty sensible." But Ruth misunderstood, as Werner pointed out: "It is not the money but your character. Where are all your promises? To your parents, your God, and to yourself. How can I say you are sensible if you keep going the way you are now? You have now been on this Job over 5 months. You have received over $800.00. What have you saved? 64 in the bank? You had more than that in cash before you ever started on that Job. No! 'Disapointed' I will say."

Amid this parental disappointment and concern, a letter addressed to Ruth arrived at the Nelson household. Lilly noticed the return address—The School of Nursing, University of Minnesota. Assuming that it was a job offer, she opened it and read instead:

Dear Miss Nelson:

The Office of admissions and records tells me that there are several incompletes in your record. I do hope you will be able to complete all of your work in order that your record may be clear. Will you let me know what you are able to do regarding your program.

Very sincerely yours,
Katharine J. Dansford
Director

In her next letter Lilly addressed the distressing news and tried to offer helpful suggestions: "Why don't you make up your mind to finish up all your work at the U. so you can get it. Drop all your social life for a while (only do what is absolutely necessary.) and clear up everything—it grieves me to think that you want to go thru life sort of slip shod in your studies etc. I wouldn't go out with any

A Nelson family picture taken in 1936 when Ruth was sixteen. From left to right (back row): Ebert, Ira, Ruth; front row: Gordon, Werner, Lilly, Hilding (Ruth's oldest sibling, who died in a gun accident before the events of this book).

young men if I were you—that Ellstrom boy—hope you have shown him that you are a Christian and not gone with him to shows."

Ruth had known for months that she should finish her degree. But with no one else aware that she hadn't actually earned it—not even her employer, the City of Two Rivers—she had found the necessary work easy to postpone. Now, with pressure from her parents to address the situation, I thought she might face her failure and deal with reality.

Instead she dawdled. One month after her father wrote to her, her parents finally heard from her—not a letter but a card. She promised that she would write a letter "in the evening." Lilly was impatient: "Your card written Fri. A.M. came this morning. If you did like you said (you would write a letter in the evening) we ought to have one tonight or to-morrow morning—hope you do—Dad sure has been waiting."

Eight more days passed before the long-promised letter arrived. Werner was disappointed at seeing "nothing in it in repply to my two letters of almost two months ago." He pressed her: "Say Ruth did you not make us believe last summer that you got your Degree and your diploma? Did you get them? If not, why did you deceive us? This grieves me." He concluded by raising the stakes: "As Long as you are only deceiving me like you do I want to have nothing to do with you—so good bye until you answer my two letters."

Writing on the same day, Lilly reinforced the message: "Your letter came today—couldn't imagine what was the matter when you promised to write the same night as you sent the last post-card. You'll have to get strict in keeping your promises or not make them."

Lilly reminded Ruth that her actions affect "not only us but Bob's folks + others [who] have done a lot for you [and are] expecting much of you—you must measure up to their and our expectations." And of Ruth's obligations to Bob himself: "If he loves you as much as he says, that is after all the most important." So, Lilly exhorted, "you ought to be true to him."

Then Lilly returned to a tired theme: "Do you remember how many times you said 'I will pay you back' to dad. I know that if you had only started he would have felt that you were keeping your promise and he wouldn't have required so much. Now he thinks you are going on with your work in the same slipshod way."

Ruth's silent inaction, Lilly added, posed ongoing difficulties for her with Werner: "When it comes to the point I couldn't tell very much because I have nothing really clear to tell, he thinks I am keeping a lot of things from him. That makes it hard for me."

Finally Ruth sent her parents a check for $200. Werner decided not to cash it "until you have more money in the bank." Repeating that the debt was only part of what Ruth needed to address, he continued: "I hope to God that you can arrouse yourself to action at once. This is a terrible dark cloud over your proffessional name. And I hope you take warning now before the storm of sorrow brakes lose over you. You may not succeed in escapeing the consequences of this sin either, but let us hope that God will grant it."

On the back of Werner's letter Lilly added: "Thanks for your letter which came Thursday eve—You mentioned the paper on Child Welfare that you had written + not finished, was it because it had something to do with your own life? Maybe we could help you with it—do write + tell us what puzzles + remember 'God helps those who help themselves.'"

Several days later Werner wrote to Ruth again, a five-pager filled with suggestions, biblical quotations, and exhortations addressing her situation: "Your most important concern is 1st to keep up your Spirit. Each day does bring its disappointment. then just settle it between you and your God—You should be able to clean up on the whole thing in about 2 months and you should enjoy doing it." He continued by speculating that prison or unemployment could result if her falsehood were found out. So she needed to "burn all the bridges to your past Sinful life and say goodbye to it. I am very eager that you succeed this time," he concluded, but if she didn't, "I have no other choice but to abandon you as hopeless and try to forget that I ever had a girl, a daughter. It was only a heartache."

However Ruth responded to her father's threat, her parents' expectations would have continued to weigh heavily upon her. I believe that their letters would have reminded her of those expectations, fed her guilt and shame, and added to her stress.

And that stress must have been considerable. Starting in the summer of 1943, Ruth failed to earn her degree and then tried to hide her failure. She took her first nursing job, saying nothing to her employer about lacking the necessary qualifications. She became pregnant and endured an abortion—stressful enough by itself, many times more so because it was illegal. When she told her fiancé what she had done, she shattered his trust. Finally she found herself threatened by legal and public exposure, given the circumstances of John Schmidt's death.

I can understand how these many stressors may have kept Ruth indecisive. Bob—who still didn't know of the academic failure—considered her next communiqué to be a "very serious letter" with "very good common sense in it." He agreed that they should "resolve between ourselves on my next leave to be serious" because "marriage is to be considered a serious step." Perhaps intending to be serious upon their next meeting would help her to decide whether to marry him.

If Ruth's outlook with Bob was murky, at least she could decide about her professional future. But she agonized over that too. If she moved back to Minneapolis to finish her degree, she could get her parents off her back and get what she needed to become a bona fide registered nurse. But she would have to do schoolwork, returning to a failure that still stung. In addition, there would have been the factor of shame. With no one other than her parents aware of her academic failure, she could keep the secret a little longer.

With no motivation to finish her degree, Ruth may have reconsidered an option she had been resisting for months—to join Bob in California. But what would she do there? Without a nursing degree she couldn't get a job as a registered nurse. So she would likely be stuck in a lower-status job or doing nothing all day long in a place where she had no friends. And she would be with a man whom she was not sure she wanted.

Instead Ruth lay low in Two Rivers. She continued to work, perhaps saved some money, and hoped that no more disclosures would surface. She could imagine that her troubles might somehow be swept away with the passage of time.

Even if she had decided what to do, at least for the time being, choosing with whom she would do it still eluded her. Would it be Bob? Stu? Russ? Greg? "that Ellstrom boy"? Someone else? No one? For all these reasons for all these months, Ruth dithered about her future—her professional future and her personal future.

Finally Bob decided that he had had enough of Ruth's indecision: "Until you've cleared matters up in your own mind regarding me, your ideas, your future, your parents, etc. we'll just forget about everything." He reminded her that "I've never been against your ideas, your future or your parents. I thought I'd conveyed the idea I was thoroughly in accord with all three." He was put off by her "constantly reminding me of your past bad luck." Apparently Ruth had speculated that Greg was so egotistical that getting her pregnant meant nothing more to him than a show of his manhood. Bob agreed, "although no man would ever admit it." Then he contrasted himself with Greg: "I'm not in love with myself in any way, shape, or manner, but, I do consider him poor competition." With Greg in the conversation, Bob decided to close "before I end up giving you the 'riot act' you sort of expected on our last meeting," the meeting, that is, when Ruth had first broken the news to him about her pregnancy. Reminded of that disheartening event, he signed off more distantly than ever: "Yours—BoB."

"The Kids Talking About You and I Getting Married"

Meanwhile Ruth and Stu exchanged Valentine's Day cards. His was a frivolous one:

> A jug of wine and thou
> Beside me in the wilderness—Would that be fun—AND HOW.

Hers was a more serious one that he praised as "to the point." She also included a "nice long letter" in which she reflected on the Schmidt tragedy and asked for Stu's understanding about why she hadn't called him when she visited Minneapolis on that dreadful weekend. Then she referred to their friends' gossip about—of all things—her marrying Stu.

Stu's reply ten days later was uncharacteristically long and reflective: "I'm glad you were in a serious mood and wrote as you did. Sometimes it helps to get things off your chest—I believe I feel I know you better because you did." About Ruth's quick trip to Minneapolis, he replied: "I know you were under quite a strain when you were here and not quite yourself. I believe, had I been in your shoes, I couldn't have done any better."

He addressed the gossip—"Yes, I have noticed, as have you, the kids talking about you and I getting married"—and he elaborated: "When we first starting going out I honestly admit I went out with you to just hear of Veronica. But we continued, even after I thought I had a chance of going back. So I knew then what a really swell person you were and the more I see you the more I think of you. As far as marriage is concerned, we neither are in a hurry it seems."

I was startled to learn that Ruth and Stu were considering marriage. If their friends were talking, their relationship must have been intense. I could understand Ruth's balking at his proposal because of her qualms about marriage. But I still had trouble with how blithely she seemed to ignore it. Or maybe not. Perhaps she simply couldn't refuse any suitor's advances. Juggling the relationships was her way of dealing with all of them.

"Ruthie, I Love You!"

Bob had cooled toward Ruth. And Stu had cooled toward the idea of marriage. But Russ kept pulling out all the stops. After he had whimsically—but, it turns out, seriously—suggested that attending Veronica's wedding with Ruth could afford them an opportunity to marry, in his next letter two days later Russ reported that her reply had come "so soon" that he was "a bit surprised." Given Ruth's dilatory style of correspondence, especially with Bob and her parents, her reply to Russ by return mail suggests that she now gave him high priority. Her encouraging letter had pleased him; in closing he promised: "As long as you insist you can bear with my boring letters I'll continue writing as often as possible."

But Russ hadn't fully opened his heart to her. Six days later he summoned all his courage:

Ruth darling, the rest of this letter may shock you a bit, but there's no getting away from it. Ruthie, I love you! I hope this doesn't shock you too much, but I'm sure that after all this time you know me well enough to realize that I'm not the type of guy who would hand any beautiful girl he met a so called line! I've thought it over a long while and I know that as far as I'm concerned you're the one girl! I know that in view of the uncertain position I'm in at present I have no right to ask you to marry me. I also know that I'm not worthy of you under any circumstance, but just to know that there was a chance, and that you'd wait till I get back and give me a chance to prove my love for you would make me the happiest man in the world. Believe me, darling, this is the first time I've ever spoken seriously to any girl and I mean every word I've said! I want you to know that whatever your reaction to this letter may be, I'll always think of you as the swellest girl I've ever met!! So, until next time, I'll be waiting for your reply & will write whenever possible.

What Russ read in Ruth's next letter "really had me worried for a while. And I do mean worried ! !" She had written not about her own wedding but Veronica's. Relieved, Russ asked if she would buy a wedding present for Veronica because Ruth's "good judgement will be, no doubt, much more practical than mine." Gaining steam, he suggested that the wedding gift for Veronica be "a gift from us." But then he hedged: "However, if you don't approve of the idea you can send it as being from me."

With his next letter Russ sent Ruth money for the present. Then he turned to a heartfelt concern:

Ruthie, dear, I hope my last few letters haven't offended or should I say embarrassed you, in any way. Maybe I had no right to reveal my feelings to you under the circumstances, but I'm sure you'll understand that it couldn't be helped + that I meant every word I said + still do. I think you know I'm not the kind of a guy who'd get a pleasure out of breaking anyone up but I do want to see you happy, if you get what I mean. And I guess, at the same time, I'm rather selfishly thinking of my own happiness too!

I could discern part of Ruth's reply by Russ's responses in his next letter. She sent him the address of her brother Ebert, also stationed in England at the time, expressing her hope that the two might meet. She also offered to send Russ whatever he needed. What she didn't do was the most significant of all—she didn't discourage his ardor.

More than three weeks had passed since Bob had written, his longest break ever. Though Ruth may have discarded or lost correspondence, the start of his next letter on April 1, 1944—"the first one in ages"—suggests that the break was intentional. He seemed to have warmed to Ruth again—addressing the letter with "Dearest, dearest, dearest Bunnie" and pleading with her not to be angry with him but then immediately changing course: "You said in your last letter that you had an idea what was wrong. Well, well, 'Smartie pants,' what is wrong?"

For once Ruth answered Bob's question, writing to him about her academic failure. The news took him by surprise, but more than that, it hurt. "I thought we were going to stay 'frank' with each other," he reminded her, but dejection overruled: "So much for that." With this setback his hope of her joining him in California plunged precipitously, as he mused: "Some anticipations never come true."

"Remember That Picture You Promised Me, Snooks?"

Then, after the long months of frustration, Bob let fly: "And another thing, if you don't get your picture soon, I'm going to come home and get it myself. I'm telling you, bunnie kid, I'm getting desparate." Though Bob had mentioned repeatedly over the years the "little picture" of Ruth that he kept in his locker or on his desk, he longed for a better one. As early as April 1942 he had asked for "a picture of you in your swimsuit." When they had met in Chicago in 1943, he had again asked her to send him a "glamour shot." Her promise to do so raised his expectations, unleashing five reminders over the next four months.

Finally, the picture appeared, but it was no glamour shot. Bundled up in a heavy coat, Ruth seems caught, not even facing the camera squarely, no smile, a harried young woman on

Ruth's unglamorous "glamour shot."

a winter day. It was a picture all right, but it wasn't the picture Bob hungered for.

Perhaps Ruth responded with that picture because of persistent stress and grief. She still hadn't finished her degree. She still worried about being exposed for working in a job under false pretenses. She still suffered from the anguish of finding herself pregnant and the aftermath of her illegal abortion. She still felt under the pall of the broken trust in her relationship with Bob—despite his continued love, he also continued to include pointed digs in his letters. And she still found herself anxious about potential fallout from the John Schmidt case. How could one so overwhelmed in so many ways even consider glamour?

"Down in the Dumps"

Ruth also continued to dither about her future. Even so, Bob still couldn't shake her. On the same evening he pleaded for her picture, he seemed ready to wait for seven years: "How long did it take Jacob to get a wife?" This note also reflects a return to his affectionate mode, evident in his sign-off: "Lovingly—Bobbie." Was he backing off his suggestion to "just forget about everything"?

Not at all. The third letter he wrote on that same April Fool's Day reveals why: "Excuse me snooks, I'm drunk." He continued: "I'm afraid you're haunting me. I just can't get over my dark haired Swede! I love you more, honey, than you'll realize." Yet in his uninhibited state he brought himself to acknowledge that the relationship was collapsing, as he took "it for granted you and I are never [going to be] married." Even so, "you will always be one girl who would always stand out in my mind. You're an ace." He closed the letter because "it's time for my Amphogel again." He took the "terrible stuff" to calm his queasy stomach, probably a symptom of chronic anxiety.

Though Bob reacted to Ruth's haunting by getting drunk, he also conjured the possibility of a proactive response: "No promises, but I hope to see you soon." A week later he had "approached the skipper" about getting a leave. A wire he sent two days later reported: "LEAVE CANCELLED LETTER FOLLOWING."

The canceled leave fed his despondent mood: "I'm really down in the dumps now that I felt I was close and now am so far." Writing on a Saturday night, when people often went out, he contemplated having "to quit being a good boy cause it looks like good boys don't get very far." Then, realizing that Ruth could misunderstand, he elaborated: "I was just wonderin how some of these guys around here do it. There's one guy who has a peach of a wife, pretty as the dickens and really an intelligent kid, and he's stepping out time + time again. Now he's laid up with [gonorrhea] and evading her for that reason—No reason for it as he claims his marital relations couldn't be better but he just likes new pasture. Now, isn't that to darn bad?"

Though he appeared to share this story as a compelling reason to stay in on a Saturday night, might Ruth have read it as a reminder of her past infidelity? His letter suggests that he thought of that possibility: "Of course, it works both ways."

Even with his leave canceled and feeling as down as ever, during the next week Bob was still hoping, writing that he "just can't wait until we're together even though as you say 'will only be for a little while.'" As if he had forgotten he had told Ruth just a few weeks previously that "we'll just forget about everything," he now pleaded with her not to leave him because "you're my inspiration."

Yet Bob knew better than to expect Ruth to make up her mind about him, at least for now. So he jump-started his plans for a transfer, writing to her in the same letter that "I may have a chance to go to Rio di Janiero on a shore job."

In the meantime the letters from Russ had abruptly stopped, Stu remained in his holding pattern, and Ruth had yet to arrive at a point where she could decide about Bob. Nor did Bob seem to be sure about Ruth. One day he had had enough of her; another day he pleaded with her not to leave him. Even if he could somehow wangle a leave and see her "only for a little while," what would he say? What could they decide? Besides, a recent exchange revealed that their bank account had no funds. What could they do with no money to spend? The prospects for a leave held little promise. The prospects for Bob and Ruth held even less. Their flickering flame was about to sputter out.

"Father Reads Ceremony"

The Wednesday, May 10, 1944, edition of the *Two Rivers Reporter* included, in the "News of Women's Activities" section, a report of Bob and Ruth's wedding.

I had known, of course, that my parents were married on May 3, 1944. Still, the tension, the suspense, and the weeks of silence leading up to their wedding put it into an entirely new light. Now

Two Rivers, Wis., Wednesday Evening, May 10, 1944

NEWS OF WOMEN'S

Father Reads Ceremony as City Nurse Weds Chief Petty Officer

The Rev. and Mrs. N. Werner Nelson of Balsam Lake, Wis., announce the recent marriage of their daughter Ruth, to Chief Petty Officer C. Robert Larson, U. S. C. G., son of M. and Mrs John A. Larson, of Minneapolis, Minn.

The double ring ceremony took place at the home of the bride's parents last Wednesday, May 3, and was performed by the bride's father in the presence of the immediate families. Following the ceremony a wedding supper was served.

The bride was attired in a white flannel suit with gold accessories and wore a corsage of gardenias and sweetheart roses. She was attended by Miss Fumee Dahlberg of Balsam Lake who wore a sky blue flannel suit with white accessories and a corsage of talisman roses.

The groom was attended by Gordon Nelson of Muskegon, Mich., brother of the bride.

The bride is a graduate of the University of Minnesota School of Nursing and is presently employed as the city public health nurse here. Chief Larson has recently returned from the south Pacific and is stationed at Morro Bay, Calif. He attended the University of Minnesota and before entering service was an engineer at Rochester, Minn.

Mrs. C. R. Larson

Last Call to Plant Victory Gardens Issued by WFA District Supervisor

Bob and Ruth's wedding announcement in the Two Rivers paper.

that I knew its context, the announcement seemed to jump out of nowhere.

Family lore had supplied me with only three facts about my parents' wedding. It was hurried because of my father's short leave. It was held in the living room of the Nelson home in Balsam Lake. And, on that spring day, snow flurries fell in Minneapolis. Family lore could not address my spate of questions. What happened during those weeks of no letters from Bob? What made him decide to make the bold move to go east? Why did Ruth agree to marry? What did her parents say? What really happened?

Perhaps Bob's seesaw feelings about Ruth during the preceding two months had set the stage for him to resolve the matter—he realized that he didn't have to wait for Ruth to join him in California. As he had angrily threatened the previous year, this time he managed to get a leave so that he could visit her and bring the matter to a head.

Here is a probable scenario:

Bob may have shown up on Ruth's doorstep in Two Rivers unannounced; the letters say nothing of any plans. The couple then spent the weekend of April 28–30 getting reacquainted. At some point he issued an ultimatum: either marry me now or we're through for good. Under the pressure of the moment and Bob's skill at persuasion, Ruth caved. County records show that on Monday, May 1, they obtained a marriage license in Manitowoc, the county seat. They drove to Balsam Lake in the city car Ruth used for her job. On the day after the wedding a Minneapolis photographer took a wedding picture. A day or two later Bob hopped a train to Morro Bay, and Ruth drove back to Two Rivers.

Here and now I see my father as a knight journeying to a distant land to claim the woman he loved. The image fills me with admiration and pride. And surprise. Before I read the letters, I couldn't have imagined him this way. I believed that he loved my mother, but his verbal expressions of that love were few. When he showed up on Ruth's doorstep in 1944, he was courageous, having overcome his anxiety and fear to settle the matter. My dad was on a knight's quest to win his princess. I could almost pretend that a happy ending was about to emerge.

But what about Ruth? The last time she had written about marriage, in a letter to Stu, she had apparently expressed profound ambivalence. Not only did she change her mind in a short time, but the man whom she married was Bob, the one who had all but broken up with her just a few weeks previously. After months of indecision what caused her to make up her mind to get married— and to Bob?

Perhaps Ruth became convinced that marriage had some practical benefits. The change in social status could lighten her many burdens. Once she was married, her parents could see her as settled down and perhaps back off. The debt she owed her father would now become Bob's too. Similarly marriage could have eased her fear of losing the Two Rivers job for which she was not qualified. She could leave it as she no longer needed to depend on herself for an income. Moreover she could give as her reason for leaving—in the 1940s, a highly acceptable explanation—that she was joining her new husband in California. In much the same way she may have seen marriage as a way to alleviate the shame that dogged her about the illegal abortion. She may have felt that, were it to become publicly known, being married would help fend off those who might question her character. Finally perhaps she had grown weary of trying to decide among her many suitors. Marrying Bob could give her peace.

While I was a senior in college with no idea what I would do with my life, I asked Suzie to marry me. My mother resisted the engagement, urging me to find my profession first. That would take years, I figured, so I rejected her advice and married anyway. Family lore about my mother's own wedding offered her no help in expressing her viewpoint, and it gave me no help in understanding it. Both Suzie and I speculated that Ruth's real resistance was to Suzie herself—an almost impossible position from which to build new family ties.

Over the years their relationship eased into cordial tolerance, each trying to get along with the other as best as she could. Still, though, I felt the discomfort hovering in the distance—between Ruth and Suzie and between my mother and me when we were talking about Suzie.

Now I know a more nuanced version of the circumstances leading up to Ruth's own wedding—that she didn't want to marry when she did because she had doubts both about Bob in particular and about marriage in general. If she had shared this more nuanced reality to contextualize her reasons for wanting me to wait, we might have connected on a deeper level. Perhaps the tension would have eased, enabling us to discuss how each of us saw my prospective marriage. The marriage itself might have gotten off to a better start, and all our relationships might have matured. Twenty-six years later, when Suzie died, Ruth might have found it easier to reach me in my grief.

Ruth's own wedding must have felt like a whirlwind, perhaps hardly real. Indeed she may have finally acted precisely because of an overall sense of unreality. She may have found it easier to marry Bob if she imagined him to be someone other than he really was. This would explain the published announcement that she wrote in which she fudged basic details about the man she had married.

Thus, according to Ruth's newspaper version, Bob had "recently returned from the south Pacific." This makes it sound as if his wartime service included combat and recent combat at that. In fact his one voyage on a transport ship hadn't even approached a combat zone and had ended nine months previously. Did she want people to assume that he had seen combat, a more dashing image than what he really did—type forms and ride a horse in California?

Ruth took further liberties in describing Bob's background and experience. She noted that he had "attended the University of Minnesota" when he had taken only a few classes at the far less prestigious Minneapolis Business College. She characterized him as an engineer, but his real job had been mechanic's helper.

Ruth had deceived those closest to her about her academic failure. She did the same to her employer. Here, in the wedding announcement, she deceived again—not one slip but several. Her actions continued to point in a direction I didn't want to go. I had used euphemisms—she fudged and she took liberties—to make the truth more palatable.

Now, I have to admit it: My mother lied. She lied about her academic failure, about her qualifications for employment, and about her personal life. She even lied about her spouse's identity. As these incidents accumulated, I could no longer see them as isolated exceptions. Instead they comprised a pattern of deception that I still find hard to reconcile with the mother I thought I knew.

I first interpreted these revelations as Ruth's rebellion against her upbringing, but that usually occurs during adolescence. However, Ruth's teen years had passed under the small-town scrutiny of Balsam Lake that was intensified by the magnifying lens of her father's preacherly role—he even delivered her high school's commencement address. So her rebellion had to await her college years, especially after she transferred to the University of Minnesota. Veiled by the anonymity of the sprawling campus, she could relax her scruples without having to worry about being seen by anyone from home. So she went to movies, dated lots of men, and partied hard—so hard that it cost her dearly.

But a delayed adolescent rebellion doesn't explain my mother's deeper moral lapses. They were matters of character. When I first tried to come to terms with them, I was struck by how sharply they contrasted with how I remembered her. What happened?

Perhaps nothing. Ruth's modus operandi always was passivity. After not finishing her nursing program, for example, she told others only when circumstances flushed her out. And even after that she wouldn't finish for more than a decade. Her well-honed skill at denial supported her passivity, as did secrecy. The longer she could keep the truth from being known, the easier it was to ignore and the easier it was for her to coast.

Parenthood could have also played a role. For the conscientious parenthood urges honesty: little eyes observe, little ears listen. Given Ruth's hypersensitivity to the perceptions of others, I believe that having observant children around led her to act more authentically than she might have otherwise. Also, she would have felt responsible for her children's character development. Perhaps wanting to steer us toward truth-telling, for our sake she repressed her tendency to deceive. In any event I had long believed my mother would never tell a lie. I thought she was perfect.

My mother thought I was too. For a long time I was a mama's boy. She pampered me and proclaimed to anyone who would listen that I was her "perfect baby." It wasn't just the long golden curls that she left on me till I was three. She kept it up as I grew, mustering what seems in retrospect to be rather scanty evidence: no cavities, no broken bones, 20/20 vision. By the time I reached high school, thankfully she had backed off a bit, but the embarrassing adulation continued lifelong.

Why perfection? I now believe that, if she could persuade herself that I was somehow perfect, I could represent an outcome that she wouldn't have to avoid. If this baby arrived with nothing to change, nothing to undo, nothing to hide, nothing to be sorry for, nothing to be threatened by, nothing to fear—if, in short, one of her outcomes actually worked out right—then she could feel justified. Projecting perfection onto me could move her beyond past imperfections.

Until I came to this point in my narrative, I hadn't realized how my mother's insistence on my supposed perfection had affected my own assessment of her. As I wrote and pondered, however, I realized that I had fallen prey to a doubly false syllogism: If my mother saw me as perfect, how could I see her as anything less? Like my father before me, I had put her on a pedestal; like Bob, too, I ultimately had to take her off and affirm her reality, flaws and all.

Our pedestals differed. My father's put Ruth in the position of a perfect princess and ideal lover. Mine instead modeled an ideal character. If asked about my mother, I would describe only her tenderness, her understanding spirit, or her earnestness about her faith. These were all truly part of her, but there were other parts as well. Not until I had read the letters did I see the need to affirm these other parts. When I took her off my pedestal, I could see this fuller portrayal included small-mindedness, smugness, and, most of all, guilt.

"Look, the Frog of God!"

I had begun to notice these traits in myself during college and graduate school as part of my own faith journey. But I didn't associate them with her, ascribing them instead to our mutual background of faith. This tradition asserts that a personal relationship with Jesus Christ is the only way to heaven—thus the small-mindedness. It asserts that one's behavior is a direct reflection of one's faith—thus the smugness. Then it connects faithfulness to perfection by asserting that being faithful means obeying the perfect will of God. Those who miss that mark can ask God for forgiveness, but if they had been sincerely seeking

God, they really should have known better to begin with. God forgives, but the sinner's guilty feeling remains because of the failure to follow God's will.

Denial is the glue that keeps this perfectionist version of Christianity from unraveling. If you can deny the extent of your sin, then you stand a better chance of *feeling* forgiven. Denial helps you to feel that your sin—especially if it was really bad—wasn't so bad after all. It keeps guilty feelings from overwhelming you; with denial at the ready you can return to trying to reflect God's perfect will through your life. Until, that is, you commit another really bad sin. Then denial steps in again to ward off guilty feelings and ultimately despair.

I was immersed in this version of Christianity from childhood. After I completed fourth grade my mother saw to it that I attended a week of summer Bible camp. At the nightly chapel service an evangelist told stories that focused on sin and the need for forgiveness, and then he instructed us to bow our heads and close our eyes. If we wanted to have our sins forgiven and to ask Jesus into our heart, we should raise our hand. "With heads bowed and eyes closed," the evangelist intoned, "I want those of you with your hand raised to make your way forward and join me at the front." Terrified, I stayed in my place for the first two nights. But the guilt kept coming, and on the third night, after peeking to make sure I wouldn't be the only one, I raised my hand. As I made my way through the darkness to go back to my cabin that night, I felt exhilarated that God had blessed me with salvation.

As I grew into adolescence, my school friends had parties where alcohol and sex were the main attractions. I liked these kids and wanted to stay friends with them. But I also believed that my Christian faith should keep me from their sins. Torn between my friends and my faith, I felt lost. And then, one evening in my bedroom, I turned to the Bible for insight into my dilemma, and

I felt found. "So everyone who acknowledges me before people, I also will acknowledge before my Father who is in heaven; but whoever denies me before people, I also will deny before my Father who is in heaven" (Matthew 10:32–33). A rush of energy hit, as if Jesus himself were speaking directly to me.

The youth group at church soon became my closest circle of friends. I helped plan and lead weekly share-and-prayer meetings and annual retreats, I preached on Youth Sunday and volunteered at a Christian coffeehouse, and I witnessed about my faith to strangers. Once I even stood up during Sunday worship to assert my view that the pastor's sermon had failed to reflect the Gospel. From the confines of my tight-knit group, I believed that Jesus was the only way to God, that the way I lived showed the strength of my faith, and that I should continue to seek God's preordained will for my life.

Ironically it was Bethel College, the small Swedish Baptist school that had sheltered my mother before her excursion into the wide-open world of the University of Minnesota, that cracked open my own world. Dr. Thomas Correll's Introduction to Cultural Anthropology course rattled my cage. Tom had worked for many years as a missionary among the Inuit before earning his doctoral degree in linguistic anthropology. He would share experiences from his years in the Arctic to show how language not only reflects but creates alternative realities, raising profound questions about the nature of truth.

Thus, for example, the difficulties of Bible translation. "Imagine," Tom began class one day, "if you had to translate 'Behold, the Lamb of God!' for Inuit speakers who have no word for *lamb*. What would you do?" A lengthy discussion ensued. What role did lambs play in the ancient Near East, and what did the gospel writer mean by having John the Baptizer call Jesus a lamb in that context? Could we transport all that to Inuit culture in the contemporary Arctic to find a functional equivalent for *lamb* in that radically different setting? I think we ended up with, "Look, the frog of God!"

This was my first lesson in distinguishing between the word of God and the words of the Bible. I could no longer cling to the idea that God had hallowed every biblical word as sacred in English, which was the version that I was reading. But I also no longer needed to feel torn between mindless faith and faithless mind; Tom introduced me to Ernest Becker's *The Denial of Death*, a book that supplied intellectual legitimacy for my faith and helped me to connect my emerging anthropological consciousness to a global Christianity.

There were other challenges. For as long as I could remember, for example, I had believed that God's will for my life was unitary, present, and immutable. It was like an itinerary somewhere in the recesses of the divine mind but one that I couldn't easily access. My duty was somehow to discern and then follow God's will. Otherwise, farewell to my hopes of being a faithful Christian.

But then I heard Professor Art Lewis speak during a chapel service. He started by claiming that he had followed God's will when he married the woman who became his wife. I leaned back, prepared for a sentimental sermon about years of marital bliss. But that's not where he went. Instead he said that he could have been just as much in God's will and just as happy had he married someone else. He probably went on to mention God's having given Adam and Eve the power to choose, but if he did, I didn't hear it. I was aghast.

If he was right, how would I know which choice for my life was *the* right one, the one ordained by God? The idea that God would allow this degree of freedom was terrifying. Terrifying but ultimately deeply freeing and profoundly energizing. No longer locked into trying to discern God's cosmic blueprint for my life,

I was free to choose from among real options, any one of which could be God's will.

If Bethel College had started to shake my foundations, Bethel Seminary gave me the tools to explore the tremors. My study of biblical Greek and Hebrew taught me that the human production of the Bible shows more evidence of divine activity than would God's supernatural intervention. I learned that to assert "the Bible says" without qualification, as did so many preachers in my youth, is disingenuous. To say, "I interpret the Bible to mean" is both more honest and more accurate. And the Jesus as "personal Lord and Savior" of my childhood faith was greatly augmented by a host of new perspectives, especially the justice-seeking Jesus as prophet.

Dizzy from my spiritual ferment, I was eager to cast out anything from my past that did not accord with my new knowledge. But Professor Marvin Anderson, my teacher for a seminar on church history, saw danger ahead. He advised: "I know you have come to disagree with the Swedish Baptist pietism you were raised in. I encourage you to try to understand where your ancestors were coming from, what they had to deal with, and how their style of faith addressed their situation. I hope that, as you throw out the bathwater of your disagreement, you don't throw out the baby of the faith which sustained them."

Perhaps this advice helped me to reject my mother's version of Christianity without rejecting my mother herself. We still loved each other and maintained a decent relationship until she died. But mostly it was another tightrope act, in part accomplished by still more denial.

But this time, while I was in seminary, I was party to the denial too. I was wary of the pietistic concern that too much thinking about God can threaten one's devotion to God. If I confided in Ruth about the changes in my thinking about Jesus, I worried, she would wonder whether I still regarded him as my personal Lord and Savior—to her that was the only true way. Because I did not want to upset our mother-son relationship, I kept quiet.

I also found that, as my understanding of Jesus expanded—Jesus as Prophet, Rabbi, Son of David, Son of God, Son of Man—I couldn't squeeze it into the identity of my "personal Lord and Savior." That identity wasn't wrong. It was just insufficient.

Although I didn't feel comfortable sharing this with my mother, once—and not until my forties—I tried to communicate my changing faith in another way. During Sunday evening services her church would sometimes offer time for testimony when people could share how they had experienced God in their life. I spoke about how I had understood God to be moving me to seek ordination, focusing on my experience of God's persistence and patience. Mom seemed to appreciate my words, though I don't recall that we discussed them afterward.

Eventually I was ordained in the United Church of Christ, a denomination that welcomes my passion for social justice and approach to faith. Still, as I moved further away from my mother's kind of faith, she never acknowledged to me that I had done so. She and Dad did attend the installation service for my first pastorate, a gesture that I much appreciated as a loving act. But she didn't tell me how she saw it. Was she affirming my new direction or was she seeing me as "my son, the pastor" without delving into details? I don't know. Our peace, to me, felt uneasy.

•

Coming to terms with Ruth's letter collection forced me to rethink my view of her and finally to approach a more realistic level of understanding. But that hasn't come easily; I am still trying to get there. Paramount among the difficulties is Ruth's consistent evasion of truth. When I first considered this unpleasant fact, I tried denial again. Ironically this bit of dormant childhood faith pushed its way forward from some cobwebbed corner within me. My denial also underscored why revising family lore has been so hard. I didn't want to concede my mother's pattern of evading the truth nor to admit that she acted contrary to my ideal image of her. But I have finally started to do so. I have come to acknowledge that my mother could and did pretend that life was the way she wanted it to be, regardless of the truth, regardless of reality. And, in certain respects, she did so her whole life long.

I remember that one day while she was driving home from work, Ruth was ticketed for turning left during prohibited hours. When she got home, she sat down at the kitchen table with the ticket, studied it line by line, and exclaimed: "Look! He wrote down the wrong time. I'm going to fight this!" She knew that her turn was illegal but found a way to undo its consequences. I had always thought of this incident as exemplifying my mother's conscientious attention to detail. Now, after reading the letters, I see it very differently. I consider the ticket incident as a muted version of Ruth's other attempts to escape the effects of her actions. Participating in her graduation ceremonies hid her academic failure. Having the abortion annulled a consequence of her infidelity. Inventing her husband in the wedding announcement obscured the real man she married. Getting her ticket thrown out voided the effect of her illegal turn. Though these actions vary considerably in ethical weight, they all represent attempts to lessen her liability for a negative outcome. For a preacher's kid scrutinized by the watchful eyes of a tight-knit community, her strategy might have made perfect sense. But it could take her only so far. It couldn't address her deeper fear of being exposed as immoral, un-Christian, or, worst of all, imperfect.

Then I tried to imagine how our relationship might have been different had Ruth affirmed her humanness and faced up to her imperfections. When I was in the throes of a third version of my doctoral dissertation and about to scuttle all hope of earning the degree, I would report my ongoing frustration in phone conversations with her. At the time I did not know of her difficulty in finishing her academic program; now I see that she could have empathized with my situation by sharing from her experience. If she had, she could have eased my burden, and our relationship might have deepened.

Her relationship with her own father might have deepened too. Early in 1945 she received a mostly warm and supportive letter from him. In closing he noted that he hadn't heard anything from her about finishing her degree. "This grieves me." Then, in the last sentence, he wondered: "Will I carry that grief with me to my grave?"

Yes, he would. Werner died ten years later; a year after that Ruth finally earned her degree. Why then? Perhaps she remembered her father's plea and was galvanized by guilt. Or maybe she received an emotional benefit from depriving her father of that satisfaction; with his death the game was over. Whatever the reason her slowness to act eleven years previously contrasted sharply with the speed of the resolution when it finally came. Even with three young children at home, she finished the degree with a summer school course. In this one respect Ruth had finally faced the truth of her failure and acted on it.

The truth of other failures, though, posed a more arduous challenge. Ruth couldn't resolve the effect of the unwanted pregnancy by taking a course. Nor could she change Bob into the man of her dreams by writing a wedding announcement. In both instances she would have had to do hard work on herself to understand the truth about her expectations and failures. So far as I know, she didn't do that. As for Bob and Ruth's marriage—well, can broken trust repair past unfaithfulness? If it can, diligent work is required. I don't believe that my parents had the tools for the

Bob and Ruth's wedding picture. Photo by Gene Garrett

job. All they could do was sputter around with "She always" or "He never."

However motherhood may have distracted Ruth, it couldn't resolve the effects of her past indiscretions on her relationship with Bob. I believe that these effects greatly contributed to the limitations I observed in how my parents interacted as a couple. When my father belittled my mother—which he did often, especially in retirement—she usually held it inside. I wanted to jump to her defense and sometimes tried to do so, no doubt awkwardly and mistakenly. When I spoke up, my father responded with a stare that I interpreted as "Stay out of this!" I never saw the interaction go beyond that point; my father would walk away in silence and my mother would mutter under her breath, "You can't change him."

Now I need to rethink my father's stare. What if I was wrong? What if he didn't intend to put me off? After all, the stare was expressionless—I never asked him what he meant by it nor did he ever offer clarification. What if the stare meant only blankness, that my father did not know what to say? Or what if it was a call for help? Or what if it was an inarticulate plea—"If you only knew"?

Now that I understand the mixed signals Ruth and Bob gave each other early on, the conditions under which their marriage started, and their failure to establish any way of working through differences, I can entertain questions like these. I can also better understand something that had always perplexed me: on the rare occasion when my mother tried to stand up to my father, her effort immediately collapsed in the face of his particularly withering look. At the time I had no idea what that look meant. Now I wonder if it bore the burden of their past.

"I Was a Little Taken Aback"

So what happened after the knight in shining armor swept his princess off her feet? The news traveled fast. Five days after the wedding Stu wrote that he had "just learned of the surprising news" and added, likely understating, that "I was a little taken aback." He assumed that now "you'll finally be able to get your trip out to Calif. this summer" and hoped that "Bob will be able to be stationed on land near you." Then, for the last time, he closed with "Well, Ruthie I was glad I knew a swell girl like you and I wish you and Bob all the happiness in the world."

Russ wouldn't have learned of Ruth's marriage for some time, as the May 2 edition of the *Minneapolis Star Journal* reported that since March he had been missing in action. In late June Ruth received a letter from Russ's mother disclosing that Russ had been taken prisoner after his plane was shot down over France. She included the address where he was imprisoned and urged Ruth to write him. Ruth jotted on the envelope that she had answered this letter on July 2, 1944. Her prompt reply is the last evidence in the letters of any connection to Russ.

"Our Plans Are Very Indefinite"

Bob couldn't rest until he had Ruth ensconced with him in California. A top priority would be housing. He had been back at Morro Bay for scarcely a week when he wrote: "If possible, let me know the date of your arrival because I'll have to arrange a place to stay." In just a few days he had investigated at least four housing possibilities and had even called the Marine Hospital in San Francisco to push a medical discharge for a sailor that, if it went through, would have opened up a "very nice little shack." But he was disappointed, not from housing possibilities that fell through but because he had heard nothing from Ruth: "I don't believe I ever raised any comment from you on the matter [of housing]." He had spent weeks working to land a place for them to live, and Ruth hadn't bothered to jot even a passing phrase in her letters about his effort. This led him to ask: "So now, dear, whose morale is low?" His answer in tiny letters whimpered: "(mine)."

When Ruth finally addressed the housing situation, she urged Bob to stop looking. After looking for more than seven weeks, no wonder his response in a June 22 letter was resigned: "Whenever you get around to leaving let me know and I'll see what I can find to settle in."

One of the houses in Morro Bay that Bob considered, with his notations.

Bob had no better luck when he explored buying a car. Ten days after the wedding he had "a 1930 Model A Ford lined up" and wrote to a former supervisor from Otis Elevator about buying his 1937 Ford coach. Bob was not content to keep Ruth on the sidelines and urged her to contact her brothers Gordon and Ira to see if they could help. Or, he wrote, she could buy a car herself. "If you got a car, say a 1936 Ford for about $150 or $200, drove it out here and we sold it for $150 or $200, we'd still be ahead wouldn't we?" As for the possibility of Ruth's encountering car trouble, Bob was blithe: "Columbus took a chance so what have we got to lose?"

Ruth replied more quickly about cars, but her response was the same—forget about it for a while. "Anything you want snooks," Bob replied, "is all right with me." Again, this struck me as more a sign of resignation than a statement of his real feelings.

In his final attempts to encourage Ruth to journey westward, Bob looked into travel by train or airplane. He even suggested a temporary solution: Ruth could join him for the summer and then return to her Two Rivers job in the fall.

I saw a familiar pattern returning. Bob was ready for their new life together to take shape. But that wasn't happening. Ruth ignored his many attempts to find housing. She told him to forget about buying a car. And she didn't respond to his other suggestions. By early June he fretted that more than a month had passed since the wedding, yet Ruth remained in Wisconsin.

And who could say when she would come? Ruth certainly couldn't because she still had to deal with several concerns. First, she had yet to devise a plan for finishing her degree. Summer school would have been a possibility, but getting time off from her job would have been tricky. What excuse could she make for attending summer school so soon after graduating?

Bob concluded that summer school would cause more problems than it solved and proposed that Ruth finish by taking a correspondence course. He followed up four days later by wondering who was responsible for setting the requirements for finishing—was it Ruth or "mostly what Miss Densford suggests?" He exhorted Ruth to leave Two Rivers so she could finish the work "in a short manner." As the days passed into weeks, the short manner Bob hoped for was lengthening considerably. By mid-June he reassured Ruth that, whatever happened, "I want you to get that sheepskin." And he repeated his suggestion about finishing with a correspondence course.

After several more weeks passed with no word from Ruth about her plans, Bob prodded: "What's the dope on your educational situation?" Then, after five more weeks and no word, Bob reminded her that "you were going to quit around August 1st and then be out here around September 1st at the latest. And during that time you were going to complete that work at the U." Apparently Ruth had suggested that she was going to finish in the Midwest—whether Wisconsin or Minnesota is unclear—before she went out to join Bob. If so, now this plan, too, was on hold.

Bob's next sentence suggests that Ruth had blamed the University of Minnesota: "They stalled you off on that and now they've stalled you another three months." But the university hadn't stalled Ruth. That February 1944 letter from the nursing school's director had been encouraging, with the expectation that Ruth would provide the initiative to finish. Somehow, though, Ruth had convinced Bob that the university was delaying her return. Was she lying, as she had on the wedding announcement? If she really didn't want to finish, then naming the university as the culprit must have seemed a perfect excuse.

Second was John's case. Given the possibility that his death had been a suicide, the insurance company that held the policy on John's life had denied payment. So his parents, beneficiaries of the policy, had sued. Since Ruth could be implicated in the events that had led to John's death, she may have felt obligated to stay in case she were called to testify. But this would risk having the illegal abortion become part of a public record. Because of that risk, even if she were to attend summer school, Bob admonished her to "stay away from John's case. Because then you'd be in Minnesota and they might want to hold you there indefinitely."

Ruth had a third reason that, she felt, kept her from joining Bob—her job. Even though she wasn't bound by a contract, she wrote, she didn't want to leave until her replacement was found. If the city had trouble finding a permanent replacement, Bob countered, it could "get along with a temporary one." Ruth also assumed that she would need to stay in Two Rivers to train her replacement. Again, Bob disagreed: "Show her your files, reports, etc., which should take about 1/2 a day. Introduce her around the other 1/2 day and then shove off. What're you going to do? Wet nurse her?"

Bob replaced *divorce* with *trip* in this cartoon while adding other elements addressing Ruth's situation.

As the weeks dragged on, Bob became resigned to Ruth's continuing to "string along" in Two Rivers while he urged her to "keep your coming out here in mind." He concluded: "Right now, our plans are very indefinite."

Ruth raised yet another reason for not coming out. She had been riding in a car during an accident that resulted in a cut to her forehead that left a small scar. Since Bob asked, "How's the head feel?" only once, it probably wasn't serious. Instead his focus turned to a claim against an insurer and how it might affect Ruth's coming out to join him. Not one to hesitate stretching the truth himself, he exhorted her "to get tough and get something from the insurance company on your scar. Remember your head hurts, you get dizzy, your hair is falling out and you can't sleep at night." He warned, "Before they get done, they'll try to have you admit it was your fault for being in the car at the time of the accident. But you stick to your guns and get all the medical support you can." After Ruth apparently had made some kind of statement for the case, Bob hoped that "your scar stood out considerably. Spose you reddened it up a little?"

The most significant impact of the accident for now, though, was whether it would affect Ruth's trip westward. Apparently she wrote in May that the claim might keep her in Wisconsin. This put Bob into a tizzy. He asked her about it six times during the next three weeks, but she "never mentioned it yet." After that he didn't mention the topic for more than two months until he asked in mid-August: "Will your coming out here create any difficulty with the scar case?" Evidently Ruth still hadn't addressed it in one of her letters to Bob.

Finally Ruth offered Bob one more reason for her continued reluctance to come west: she simply didn't feel like traveling. Bob retorted: "You're going to take one more trip—and don't you forget it!"

A Good Idea?

The uncertainty of Ruth and Bob's marital future wasn't uncommon during these years. World War II was stealing people's time and ripping apart lives. For many, marriage provided a sense of security amid the chaos. But this didn't mean that marriage was always a good idea.

Had Bob and Ruth's marriage been a good idea? These early signs were not encouraging. From the beginning separation marked their relationship. They had never lived in the same community even after they married. When they did see each other, it was for very short periods. As with so many wartime couples, theirs was a relationship of moments together between eons apart. While they dated in Minnesota, the separations lasted only a week or two. After Bob joined the Coast Guard, though, the couple met only three times—once quite briefly—before the May 1944 wedding. On that day, while the calendar showed that they had been acquainted for almost three years, they had spent little more than three weeks together. They barely knew each other.

The couple tried to overcome the long separations by exchanging letters. Yet, however valuable an epistolary relationship may be for later generations, it has daunting flaws if you're trying to live in it. First, experiencing someone through a letter pales in comparison to the richer experience of a face-to-face encounter. When you interact in person, you have access to more kinds of information. You can hear, for example, the inflection of spoken words. Or you can see folded arms signaling hesitation or a smirk indicating sarcasm. As useful as letters can be, they are unable to convey the complexities of human communication.

This limitation of written correspondence also makes ascertaining truth more difficult. Listeners can assess a statement using multidimensional sources of information such as verbal inflection, nonverbal cues, and the social situation. But a reader of letters can use only words on a page.

Likewise, written correspondence makes in-depth sharing more difficult, especially about contentious matters. The intense give-and-take needed for such conversations doesn't lend itself to a written medium. Given the many times that Bob expressed the need to discuss a matter "when we see each other next," he was painfully aware of this difficulty. He even joked that he couldn't wait to be with Ruth "so we can argue." He repeatedly raised issues and concerns that he wanted to discuss with Ruth; those discussions were repeatedly postponed.

Because Bob and Ruth married when they didn't know each other well, I believe that each wed an impression of whom each hoped the other person would be. This may explain why Ruth felt free to misrepresent Bob in the wedding announcement. Seeing him primarily as an impression, she could invent the truth in order to more closely approximate the man she dreamed of marrying. That dream man was fun-loving with a dash of naughtiness, characteristics that Bob indeed embodied. But she also dreamed of a man with an education. Having barely graduated from high school, Bob knew of this deficiency as he wrote of his need for "the education you said I should get after this war."

Ruth also wanted a man who used proper English—perhaps, for example, a man who displayed Russ's graceful diction. Bob was well aware that "my use of improper English gets you." Indeed he heard about it often enough to correct himself with a touch of sarcasm: "Am missing you agin, or should I say, 'again' before you bounce on me for misspelling a word." He asked her to excuse his use of "huh?" which he, like many other writers of the time, used to end sentences. And he asked whether he had "any other disagreeable factors or traits in my disposition or make-up." He sought this assurance, even after they were married, because "I know I'm not worthy of your love."

Bob's sense of unworthiness filled his letters. When he expressed a strong feeling—such as "going nuts about this place" or "really feeling down" or "feeling desperate" that plans remained undecided—he would follow with, "Don't take the above as scolding" or "I didn't mean to be sarcastic" or "please excuse my harping." Or, when he confessed that "I like to give you heck," he followed with, "don't let it bother you." Another time he hoped that she wouldn't "be disgusted with this dry letter." Again, he asked to be excused for "screwy ideas" and forgiven "for 'smartin off.'" Reporting that a trip to San Francisco might keep him from writing for a day or two, he cautioned himself to "knock off this baloney before you get angry with me." When that trip happened and he hadn't written for a few days, he implored: "Just couldn't get near a mail box, honey. I know it sounds a little odd but it's the gospel truth." But none of those expressions was unusual or offensive; none suggested the need for forgiveness. So why did Bob denigrate himself and so often? Perhaps his self-flagellation arose from his sense of falling short of Ruth's expectations, so he pummeled away in frustration. Or maybe he thought that she valued self-deprecation, so he did it to satisfy her. To me he comes across as so diffident that he probably accomplished little more than confirming his inadequacy in Ruth's mind. In trying to address his perceived weaknesses, he ended up highlighting them.

Yet who doesn't lack confidence sometimes, especially when as stretched and stressed as he was? And who wouldn't feel inferior if the person of your heart's desire was the paragon of perfection—a "Venus with arms," a "little dream girl," and "the most wonderful little wife in the whole world," all rolled into one? Ruth's larger-than-life persona both dazzled and dizzied him: "Gee darling, I just can't get over how wonderful and beautiful you are. It's nothing you can put your finger on, it just seems to radiate in your whole being—Your actions, your appearance, your manner, your speech—your looks, honey, I just can't explain it. It's just you! Everything you do and say is exactly the way it should be."

No wonder, then, that Bob wrote of Ruth's "getting to be an obsession" and in another letter called her "a wonderful obsession!" Months later she was "still my obsession." Yet, while he gushed about her perfection, he knew he wasn't perfect. Fully cognizant of his "faults to correct," he hoped that "someday you'll be proud of me."

But the woman Bob had put on a pedestal had broken his heart. She had dated other men, gotten pregnant, lied, and persisted in keeping them apart. Now wed, could she embrace marriage and settle down? Would she be able to win back Bob's trust? With the vigorous return of old patterns, I was skeptical.

"Wondering Why You Hadn't Answered"

To make the marriage real, Bob knew that they needed to be together. During just their first month of marriage, he repeated this desire in eight letters. In the ninth he resorted to figurative language: "You know, hon, love is something like a flower, it has to be taken care of and protected and a little frost can do an awful lot of harm. Time can sometimes be considered a frost so let's not let to much of it come along, huh?"

From Bob's perspective too much time had already passed. Ruth had sent him a quotation about forgiveness, probably asking him to forgive her delay. He replied that "your quotation is all right," but "if you don't hurry it up you won't be forgiven very easily. And I'm not kidding."

Then Bob's expectations shifted. A letter of May 29 shows the shift actually taking place: "I told [my commanding officer] that I wanted to keep a shore billet now that my wife was ~~soon~~ contemplating coming out." Bob's cross-out demoted Ruth's imminent arrival; now she was only contemplating the trip. At this point their old pattern of correspondence had returned. Marriage had been unable to change it.

During the next month or so Bob became distraught. Had Ruth, he wondered, been receiving his letters? Plowing on, he urged her to try harder to leave. She took umbrage. He replied contritely

that "I know you're trying your best to get away" and confessed
his impatience. When she wrote that she would come out as soon
as she could, he again backed off: "Yes, Yes, I know, you'll be out
here soon. And I love you for it."

Bob began to see signs of how Ruth's delay was affecting him.
Aware that "this place's driving me nuts," he pushed her yet again:
"So, what are you going to do? Stay back there or come out here?"
The uncertainty expressed itself physically. He was "taking mineral
oil now because of my irregular diet and constant fretfulness on
not knowing what to do with myself." And it affected his plans: "If
you're seriously considering staying back there then I'll be moving." That is, if she didn't join him first. Then, "If you come out
here to California, what will you do if I ship out, return to the
middle west or stay here in California? Or haven't you given it
any thought?"

Apparently Ruth had not. By the end of June, with still no word
from her, Bob decided that "maybe it would be better if you held
off coming out for a while." He quickly retracted this suggestion,
but the deep sadness in his letters continued.

And no wonder. Ruth not only delayed telling Bob about her
plans, she also ignored his requests. He asked for her schedule at
least weekly for more than fourteen weeks. He asked in vain; no
letter indicates that she responded. He kept "wondering why you
hadn't answered any of the questions."

Bob's relationships with his service mates provided another
source of tension, a further reminder that he and Ruth were out
of sync. He reported that Barney, fifty-six years old and a mentor
to the younger men, was "starting to hold a club over my head"
until Ruth came out. The doctor "asked me again when you were
coming out." And the skipper "was questioning me when you were
going to be out here. He seemed to think it took you an awful long
time. You know me, I agreed with him." Even the cook "asked me

when you were coming out. I told him in a month or so—He said that I'd told him that about three months ago." So Bob lamented: "Woe is me—I take a beating around this burg." The beating included doubts about his role in the marriage: "Everyone is asking me who wears the pants in our family. I do but I guess you tell me when to put them on, huh?"

If everyone was asking Bob when his wife was coming, hardly anyone would have been asking Ruth when she was leaving. With available nurses in exceedingly short supply, her employer would have wanted her to stay until a replacement was hired. And, with her summer duties lighter, she had more time to relax and enjoy the weather. Why would she leave when life was good where she was, especially if she was having second thoughts about her marriage?

Something else may have given Ruth pause. Bob had once assured her that he hadn't told Wally and Donna about her abortion, but then he had confided to them all the details of her legal troubles. [*What else do they know?*] Bob had also written about how often his mates needled him about Ruth's arrival. [*What do they think of my delaying tactics?*] Over and over he had told them that she was the very pattern of perfection. [*What if I don't measure up?*] Her preacher-kid antennae would have perked up—would this be another situation in which people would be watching her judgmentally? If so, this would have given her more reason to delay her westward journey.

"I Do Think Our Marriage Should Be a Bit More Possessive Than You Make It"

Bob found Ruth's ongoing silence and indecision troubling enough, but something else bothered him even more: the question of fidelity. Ruth asked whether he had gone out with another woman. He denied it, "Mostly because it wouldn't be right and proper and I don't care to," and then he scolded: "But you better get out here because people are human, don't forget." Several weeks later, when Ruth questioned him again, he remained firm: "No, that gal hasn't been after me either." Then he elaborated: "I haven't even looked at another female since we were married. Whoa, that's really something, huh?"

Ruth's doubts about Bob's fidelity may well have been driven by her own thoughts of dating others. Certainly she mentioned the possibility, because Bob shot back: "About your going out—I don't approve!! No, I don't like to have you go out—Fact is, I disapprove very much—And fact is again, I'll slap heck out of you if you do! Tough, ain't I? Ho ho—But just the same, you'd better not. Or else I'll do the same—So that's settled, huh?" In a later letter he summarized: "I do think our marriage should be a bit more possessive than you make it."

Bob figured that he had good reason to make that point. Ruth had written to him about a friend whose husband had been un- faithful, advocating that the friend should "stay with her guy" de- spite his lapse. "Why should she stay with her guy," Bob retorted, "when you don't. That isn't fair, is it? You're a great one, you are." Then, as usual, he backed off: "But I love you for it, hon."

Bob found Ruth's position about extramarital relationships both troubling, because he disagreed with her, and confusing, because she held a double standard—she could date, it seemed, but he couldn't. Bob didn't let the matter rest, closing a letter soon after with "Your faithful and loving husband." He had underlined *faithful* twenty-three times.

When I first began reading Ruth's letters, I readily responded to the stories that conformed to family lore about my father. These were the parts describing his untamed experiences, such as when he would go out for a night on the town or when he worked the system to his advantage. What surprised me was the extent to which Bob's letters flatly contradicted family lore. I had started out naively expecting that the portrayal of my father through his letters would match the lore that I had uncritically absorbed. Quite the contrary. I soon found myself having to entertain aspects of his character and his experiences that I had never imagined possible. As one surprising discovery led to another, my notes filled with exclamation points and question marks.

My understanding of my father began to shift radically. After his introduction to military life—the bar girl episode and some raucous carousing now behind him—he wrote story after story, not about *going out* but about *staying in*. Admittedly the relative lack of anecdotes about wild behavior could have been his way of trying to satisfy Ruth's doubts about his character generally. If that were true, though, why would he include such tales at all? Yet the letters are filled with stories that show him in a less-than-perfect light. No, I believe that he learned his lesson from the bar girl episode and that his Coast Guard years saw my father transform into a responsible man.

In fact Bob himself drew deeper significance from his practice of staying in, another marked departure from family lore. He stayed in not just to avoid trouble or to get more work done; he stayed in to make a moral statement. Staying in was "being good." He wrote repeatedly of being good; he repeatedly urged Ruth to do likewise. He was proud "that I don't hang around with the rest of the wolves" and wore his nickname "Lone Wolf" like a badge proclaiming his commitment and faithfulness. Again, his earnest devotion touched me.

Bob probably was not exaggerating about the extent of his fidelity. Recalling their wedding night in Minneapolis, he "came across those 'peacocks' left over since the King Cole" and "gave them to Don." If Bob had been sexually active with other women, he wouldn't have given away his condoms.

As much as Bob settled the question of fidelity in his own mind, he couldn't know if Ruth had settled it in hers, and the uncertainty plagued him: "Now tell me, have you been out on a date since [our wedding on] May 3rd? Have a hunch you have, is my hunch right?"

"How Am I Going to See If Our Marriage Will Be Happy When I Don't See My Honey?"

The spouses responded to their marriage very differently. When Bob had returned to Morro Bay after the wedding, he had shared his excitement so that "all the boys have been congratulating me left and right." And again: "The boys say married life gets better year after year." And yet again, joshing: "Everyone's been telling me how lucky I am to be married. And then when I show your picture they can't figure out what's wrong with you. Marrying me, I mean."

Ruth shared little of this excitement. Writing a month after the wedding, she wondered whether she should have married at all. "I can understand why you should feel like that sometimes," Bob responded, "but just stop and think, snooks, ten years from now you wouldn't care to be an old maid that people would invite out only because of sympathy." Her concern, though, ran deeper than the impact of a hypothetical future spinsterhood. She appeared to have a genuine case of buyer's remorse and likely worried that marriage would take away her freedom. If Bob picked up on that, he made light of it: "I could see my freedom winging it's [way] upward and away, like a prisoner inside the prison walls and looking through the bars to freedom with a dove flying away. Ho, ho."

But Ruth couldn't joke about freedom, because she fretted about losing it. In a letter of July 3 Bob's point-by-point replies to her comments suggest a conversation in which she continued to resist marriage. From Bob's actual responses I could discern her concerns:

Ruth: *I don't want to lose my freedom to do as I like. I don't want to be tied down.*

Bob: Your ideas that married life ties a person down are a bit confused or misdirected, don't you think? I've always gone on leave to see and be with you and it's always been out [of] my free will and I've always enjoyed every second of it but if it'd been forced on me I'd [have] pushed back against it. That's the way I want it with you and I. When we're together it'll be because we want it that way. But your remark about Freedom makes it sound like we aren't, or that you don't, even consider ourselves as married.

What was all this about marriage and freedom? Though Ruth didn't seem to have been passionately committed to nursing as a career, she was indeed committed to a level of freedom that she hoped to achieve through marriage—which today we might well view as ironic. After she married, she wrote that "I wouldn't have to work," even though "one can never tell how handy it would be sometime to be able to." Though she anticipated working while married—"I'd like to now while we're so short of nurses"—the option remained on hold for many years.

World War II brought women access to jobs that before the war had been reserved for men. The surging wartime marriage rate shows that marriage still held great appeal for women, but the war had called its economic value into question. What woman needed a husband's income when she could have her own?

Perhaps Ruth's flailing about was her strategy for traversing the shifting sands of wartime marriage. Clearly she continued to regard marriage highly, but she also feared it as a threat to her freedom. Her struggle may explain why she and Bob discussed neither the 1942 engagement nor the 1944 marriage in their

letters beforehand. These events just happened; Bob presented himself in person and with all the persuasive force that he
could muster. In both instances she yielded to the power of the
moment.

Both events were followed by significant second thoughts
on Ruth's part. After the engagement, released from the direct
force of Bob's personality, she apparently removed the ring and
embarked on a series of flings that I believe reflect turmoil in
the face of an engagement that she now doubted. Similarly,
after the wedding and again away from the direct force of his
personality, she embarked on a series of actions that I believe
amount to delaying tactics to ward off the reality of a marriage
that she now doubted. Both times her decisions to commit were
followed by profound vacillation.

I don't know whether my mother ever fully resolved her doubts
about marriage. I can say, though, that to me she seemed most
content in the 1960s when she worked as a school nurse, her first
job outside the home since Two Rivers. She took pride in her crisp,
white uniform and the dedicated service that it symbolized. I could
sense that she enjoyed working while also a wife and mother. Now
that I am aware of her struggles much earlier in her life, I wonder
if this fulfilled a long-deferred hope.

Ruth had expressed other concerns.

Ruth: *I'm worried that marriage might change you. You'll quit being nice to
me and turn into a cranky old husband.*

Bob: No, dear, I don't feel that now that we're married I'm going
to quit being a good guy and become a cranky old husband. Fact
is, I've been hoping that you'd slide off the dime and would be
out here quicker than you realized and we could really start our
married life.

Ruth: *But then I wouldn't get your letters anymore. Your most recent ones are so full of love—have you been copying them out of books or something?*

Bob: So, so, so—you think I write love letters out of books, huh? You're wrong but I'll tell you how it came about when you get out here. But they didn't come out of a book. Is that clear?

Ruth: *You don't seem to understand that girls can sense when things aren't quite right. Girls are lovers in a different way than fellows are.*

Bob: So girls are lovers in a different way, huh? Well, I'd like to have you explain that to me. I thought I had girls pretty well figured out.

Ruth: *Well, a girl wouldn't force her point of view on a fellow like you tried to do to me at Bucky's party.*

Bob: No, that Sunday at Bucky's you were determined, fact is, you frightened me. I thought right then and there that we were going to have trouble.

The question of her delay in moving west continued to haunt their conversation.

Ruth: *By the way, I probably won't be able to come out for another couple of months or so. Is that all right?*

Bob: Honestly honey, a couple of months will be to long. I know that unless I have a ball + chain around here I won't be here. Darn it anyway—If I thought it would've taken this long—we'd probably have waited to get married, too.

Ruth's reluctance was wearing Bob down. He "didn't realize it was going to be this long a separation when I said 'I do' that night." The "separation has seemed like ages" because "the last two months have passed so very slowly." Even more troubling, he was beginning to believe that she was choosing to stay away, a clear signal of her hesitancy about marriage itself: "We could get along famously," he wrote in early June, "but if you can't possibly come or are in a mood where you'd rather not come then you're the boss." For now, anyway, he tried to convince himself that "it'll be all ok when you do arrive."

In reality all wasn't okay, as Bob acknowledged: "How am I going to see if our marriage will be happy when I don't see my honey?" He must have wondered whether, despite her wearing a wedding band, anything else had changed. As if in a dream, marriage had drifted beyond his grasp. He could only imagine what it might be.

His letters reflect these musings. He expressed hope to Ruth that "neither of us pass the infatuation stage unless we pass into it deeper." But when he asserted that "we've never yet had harsh words," he realized, "that seems odd, too, doesn't it, snooks?" Still, he concluded that "I doubt if we ever will have them." Nevertheless he proposed a penalty for future fights: "After we set up house-keeping, the first one of us who starts an argument will have to do mess cook detail alone for a week, huh?" Without being able to exchange "harsh words" in person, they were left to do so through letters, as Bob confessed: "Did I ever tell you that I always look at the end of your letter first to see if you sign it with kind words. In that way I can tell whether to expect kind or harsh words thru out the letter." But this still struck him as odd. Clearly they lacked tools for dealing with differences.

Their separation affected how they expressed other feelings, as Bob chided: "So you're starting to tear letters up on me, huh? You know I understand your moods so let's let 'em come through, eh?" He assured Ruth that she could freely express herself because "your tantrums wouldn't have much effect on me." When she claimed that "patience is a great virtue," he retorted, "Well, with you I'll have plenty," which I took to be generous until he added that "usually slow people get under my skin." In another letter, when Bob was trying to impress upon Ruth that "you can't trust anyone anymore now days," he wrote in a provocative postscript that "some people find it difficult to trust their husbands with all these beautiful gals running around out here."

"I'm Getting at My Wit's End"

As the separation dragged on, Bob became more and more forlorn. He reported that he had returned from shore duty on horseback, and "I was taking it easy and looking at all the people with their gals, kids, and what have you, laying on the beach, wading in the surf, or laying in the sand dunes and boy I got lonesome." What "gets me down is the fact that we're both in the states and can't swing" getting together. A joke in the third week of June—"If I meet you at the station with my finger thumbing my lower lip and uttering strange noises don't be surprised"—became serious by the end of July—"I'm going nuts without you," a phrase he repeated in several later letters. Lying on his bunk one night, Bob "started thinking of you and all the things you do, etc., and darned if I couldn't have bawled I got so lonesome."

Concerned that Bob would "lose his charm," two of his mates decided to do something about it, as Bob reported afterward:

> Sorry hon, I hung one on last night—woe is me—Three of us, Humphreys, Myers, and myself. First we went to San Luis for chow mein, then to Pismo, then to Santa Maria, then back to

Pismo. In Pismo I removed my shoes & stockings, lost the keys
to Humphrey's car and paraded around the town for 3 hours—
(midnite to 3 AM) We found the car keys in the car, and returned
to the base. I thought for sure I'd make the brig but didn't. You
can imagine what a fine looking Chief I was. Entered the base
with 1 shoe lost, barefooted, cap reversed, tie crooked. Everyone
vowed they're goin to tell you when you get out so that's perhaps
why I'm mentioning it now. But never again—And no, there were
no wimmin along—Strictly stag–.

The night of self-destructive activity did nothing to lift Bob's
"blue mood." Knowing that "a couple of days with me in the dumps
I can lose everything I've worked to build up," he demanded that
Ruth "be here to keep my morale up." He was "damn lonesome for
the best gal in the world." He knew that profanity would offend
her; perhaps it would also motivate her. "Without you," he concluded, "I'm at my wit's end. I'm lost." A week later he reiterated,
"I'm sorry, but I'm getting at my wit's end" and added: "It's just like
taking ice cream from a baby. You're the ice cream and I'm the
baby. Can't you just hear me scream?" By early September he had
reached the edge: "It's been so long I don't know how it feels to
be a husband."

"Please Read This with an Open Mind"

The long hours Bob worked served only to increase his loneliness. Work could distract him for a while, but the loneliness
returned the moment he went off duty. A merciless dialectic
set in—the lonelier he felt, the more he worked; the more he
worked, the lonelier he felt. The remedy for this disheartening
situation, he figured, would come only when Ruth joined him.
But when would she come?

Ruth wrote a letter in early September that came close to answering that question. Excited, Bob responded by underlining passages in red, assigning a different number to each, and then commenting according to the numbers. He mailed both letters. Together they reflect the closest approximation I have to an actual conversation between them.

Ruth wrote to convey to Bob "one thing I'm considering as far as the trip out is concerned." She began with an exhortation: "Now for goodness sakes—don't go broadcasting this around as it's one thing I'm very ticklish and sensitive about, cuz I'm awfully ashamed to think I made such a mess of my last quarter at school. (A average in high school and probably a B average the first 2 years of college) and then I go and flunk one subject and get an incomplete in another."

So she asked him to "please read this with an open mind, huh, dear?"

Ruth continued: "As you know, I have some studying to do until I can get my degree. I won't be able to work in Calif. if I don't finish this work. And I have been trying to work on it but with a job to take care of I can't get at it at all, it seems," a situation that made her feel "awfully ashamed." "I'll find clothes to fix and hundreds of other things to do instead and I don't really mean to be that way." Now that she was married, however, "I wouldn't have to work as far as that goes but one can never tell how handy it would be sometime to be able to and I'd like to now while we're so short of nurses anyhow."

"Most important of all," she wanted to finish so "I can face my father again with a clear conscience." Otherwise "he won't have any faith in me." She concluded her first point: "So that's settled, isn't it—that I'm going to finish it for sure."

The next question up for discussion is when. I wish I could've gotten it done this summer but you know how that is—working all day—you don't like to sit down in the evening again. Besides I was out in the sun as much as I could be because I thought I needed it. Well—anyhow, I didn't get it done and now I still have to plow on it. (For this I could kick myself again + again but I'm just a dummy in some ways.) I couldn't leave and go to summer school as I had plenty work to do here which I also had to get done. Naturally, it would be much nicer if I could be all thru with it before I came out and then you + I could really go on a honeymoon without a care in the world.

Then Ruth proposed what she termed a solution. In October she would ride to California with the county nurse who was relocating there. In the meantime Ruth would go to Minneapolis, stay with Bob's parents—who "would understand, I'm sure"—and "do nothing but study. If anyone asked how come I wasn't going sooner, I'd have the perfectly good reason that I'm getting a ride out on Oct. 15th and have it all planned that way. I'm sure I could get done in less than a month's time." Her plan seemed foolproof until she observed: "As I'm writing this, I'm thinking about how awful those days would be and I wonder if I could stand it."

So Ruth proposed an alternative plan:

I'd go out as soon as I'm clear here and have been in Mpls. for only a couple days—long enough to have the shower on us, etc. Then I'd study like the dickens out there and here's what you'd have to do. Keep after me til I finished and I mean it would really be a job for you to do just that. We'd maybe have to eat some of our meals out until I finished and just concentrate on my awfully dull lessons in Sociology, etc. What I'm worried about there is that you'd probably be nagging me to get them done and I'd maybe get mad at you and we'd fight about that then. On the other hand you might be able to help me a lot and we might not argue about it and I'd get done quicker and we'd have had that time together.

It will be just as hard for me to stay in Mpls til 10/15 as it will be for you to wait for me as I hate studying and I hate being away from you that much longer, too.

Then, as she was "thinking this whole thing over," she realized that "it's probably one of the reasons I have worried about going out to Calif. I'm afraid I'll not get it done if I get out there first. And I want to get it out of the way once and for all or die trying." So which plan would it be, I wondered, stay in Minneapolis and finish or go to California and probably not finish?

"You'll Have to Make the Decision for Me"

Despite his debilitating loneliness, Bob had no difficulty endors-ing the stay-in-Minneapolis option, as he tried to persuade Ruth: "You'd be close to the U and the Library for anything that might come up. It would be best if you cleared it up completely before you came out here because we'll never do it out here."

Then he brought up economics: "If I go back to school I'll get $500 per year for tuition and $75 per month for subsistence, so if you are a RN then you can be making more money than if you were just a grad." He saw this option as contributing to "our best mutual benefit." He understood that she might not be working in California but still pointed out that "you never can tell what the circumstance will be and you may as well be among the top rather than in the mass. You've got the stuff to do it so that's why I'm going to see that you do it."

As if recalling Ruth's track record, he shifted to strong words: "If you don't complete your work in that month's time you may as well figure on staying there until you do complete because if, at the end of that month's time, you tell me you can't do it then I'll be gone, I'll be shipped out." To avoid this prospect he urged that "we've got to get that extra money somehow" and elaborated that if she "can't get it through higher contemplated earnings then I'll have to get it through the extra 20% for sea duty. And that won't do. We just have to be together."

After Ruth presented her two alternative ways of finishing her degree, she punted: "You'll have to make the decision for me when to come out cuz I don't know what to do." So Bob decided. She should promptly finish the degree and then come but with a caveat: "There's not John around or Greg, is there? I want a definite answer on that last question, pronto. If he is around, I want to see you out here immediately. Just a matter of principle."

The issue of extramarital relationships wouldn't go away. Ruth knew it as a hovering specter: "As far as other men are concerned—I haven't been bothered at all. No one has touched me since you did last and I will always be faithful to you now—I know. Sometimes I think you might be worrying about that but you don't have to at all." Bob responded that he "never worried about it," but based on how he responded earlier in the same letter, I didn't believe him. He was still as worried as ever.

Then she observed, "I've always been stalling, it seems. First on getting married, now on coming to Calif. and you'll find I'm great on stalling when it comes to doing those lessons too." As she concluded the letter, she urged Bob to "be patient with me this once more." Yet, he had been married now for four months and was getting nowhere—did he have any patience left? And would she buckle down and finish or would she continue to be "great on stalling"?

The answers to both questions came in unexpected ways. Having asked him "to make the decision for me" and having promised to be "a real obedient wife for a change," Ruth received clear instructions from Bob to stay in Minneapolis and finish her degree. She did neither. Instead she telephoned him.

The phone call left Bob "in a dead sweat" because of "nerves." Ruth had rejected his advice and would join him around September 23. What had changed the plan? Ruth probably told Bob that she couldn't do it. A few days previously she had observed that the Minneapolis plan made her think "how awful those days would be and I wonder if I could stand it." It wasn't that she wouldn't do it; she *couldn't* do it. Bob must have been empathetic because they settled on a plan, even as he resumed his customary exhortation that she not stay in Two Rivers too much longer.

At first I shared Bob's empathetic response. Ruth had been through a lot, and having to finish what had brought her such shame would have demanded a Herculean effort even under the best of circumstances. She was spent and couldn't muster the strength to return to something that seemed more repulsive with each passing day.

Then I reflected some more. Once again Ruth had promised to do one thing and then did another, with Bob caught in the middle. Just as she did during the engagement, here she was, promising one thing and doing something else. I imagined Bob had seen her refusal as a rebuff, its sting eased only by the prospect of her imminent arrival.

Finally I learned why Ruth finally dropped her resistance to going west. The September 14 edition of the *Two Rivers Reporter* announced that a new city nurse had been hired. Ruth would have known this when she called Bob. I believe that it inspired her to call because now she couldn't use her job as an excuse to stay in Two Rivers. And her other option—Bob's plan that she live with his parents and finish her program in Minneapolis—was untenable because she couldn't imagine doing it. So she had no other place to go. Going west was the last resort.

I wanted to think that Ruth went west because she came to her senses, realized that she needed to face the reality of her marriage, and wanted to start a new life with Bob. But I couldn't do that. Given the context of the phone call, I don't think that her trip west was a sign that she had resolved her doubts about the marriage. No, she was being strictly pragmatic. Going west was better than going to Minneapolis.

Snubbed or not, Bob would have been ecstatic that Ruth could leave Two Rivers according to schedule, just as he had written. His hope that they could be together was about to come true.

But not quite. Ruth had to get around one last roadblock before leaving. She had been summoned by the U.S. District Court in Milwaukee to answer questions at a deposition on September 21 in connection with the Schmidt family's lawsuit against the Equitable Life Assurance Company.

The summons was the last straw. An October letter from Ruth's usually stern father described her reaction: "When we got home from Mpls, you sat down sobbing under the big pine." He remembered "every word you said. I will never forget it. It moved me so deeply. Every time I think of it, I pray for you." She likely let it all spill out—getting pregnant the previous summer, the abortion, how the Schmidts' lawsuit threatened her, the indescribable anguish. Werner reflected that "it was then I decided to go with you to Milwaukee" and "do all I could to save you from disrepute."

Whenever I had asked my mother about Grandpa Nelson—I didn't remember him; he died when I was two years old—she consistently described him as stern with a soft heart. His stern side came through loud and clear in his letters—so stern that I wondered if my mother had been thinking wishfully. Where was the softness? But here, with his letter describing his daughter's finally pouring out her heart, he responded as family lore had taught me to expect. I didn't need to modify my understanding of family lore about Grandpa Nelson.

At the September 21 deposition, with her father at her side, Ruth refused to answer questions. In his October letter Werner wondered whether they had adopted the right strategy. "But we do not know, and didn't know then—and we can never know. We did the best we could."

Though Ruth's refusal to answer questions may have kept self-incriminating information from being more widely known, her tactic complicated the situation. One way or another the adversaries in the lawsuit were likely to seek an order from the court requiring her to answer. Would she be summoned again? Would she end up in contempt? Would authorities pursue her to California or even see her trip west as an attempt to escape the jurisdiction?

The last letter in the box from Bob to Ruth is dated September 15, her twenty-fourth birthday. Realizing that "a beautiful, darling, little swede" would "be here in another week" made him feel content and "happy like." Instead of concluding his letter with sentiment, though, he shared sad news: "A kid we used to go around with was killed in the South Pacific, a good kid. One of the genuine red blooded kids the public likes to hear about. He'll be just one less in the post war era, too bad."

Then Ruth went west.

•

Since Bob and Ruth had no need to write letters to each other after she joined him in California, I can only speculate as to the date she arrived. She didn't leave Wisconsin earlier than September 21, the date she appeared at the deposition in Milwaukee. Since her father also attended the deposition, she likely accompanied him when he returned to Balsam Lake, perhaps spending a day or two there before visiting friends and her in-laws in Minneapolis.

Then, by late September or early October, she departed, probably by train, for San Francisco.

Bob had perfected his skill at working the system. Within days of Ruth's arrival he was reassigned to the U.S. Coast Guard District Office at the corner of Bay and Powell in San Francisco. Then he found an apartment at 815 Pierce Street, not far from the office. He was just where he wanted to be.

A Honeymoon?

Five months after their wedding Ruth and Bob were reunited. I can imagine their feelings of relief. Bob would have felt relieved of his chronic loneliness and thrilled that face-to-face married life was finally beginning. Ruth would have felt relieved of her troubles back in the Midwest. With the many miles separating Wisconsin from California, she may have felt that her legal difficulties were as good as over.

The reunion brought challenges. The newlyweds' relationship no longer remained on hold—an abstraction, a distant hope, a matter-in-waiting. Now that they were together, their marriage became real in a way they had yet to experience. Before, they had never lived in the same community, much less in the same household. Now, if they were to grow into their marriage, they would have to face all the vagaries of life together in the present. They could no longer "write a lot a things and then let 'em hang in mid air" or postpone concerns to "when we see each other next time." "Next time" had passed; "now" had come.

They would also have to get real with each other. For years Bob had idolized Ruth, treating her as a goddess who could do no wrong. Ruth had idealized a man of her dreams and perhaps hoped that Bob might grow into the role. For their relationship to mature, each partner had a different task. Bob would need to trade his obsessive idolizing for recognition that his "Venus with arms" wasn't a goddess after all. Ruth would need to discard the roseate dream of an ideal husband and learn to love her real one, warts and all. In short, he had to take her off an idealized pedestal; she had to put him on a realistic one.

But that task would be complicated by the burdensome baggage that each brought to the marriage. Ruth lugged in a load of guilt: While engaged, her infidelity had led to a pregnancy and illegal abortion. She had failed to finish her nursing program and then had deceived Bob and everyone else about it. She still owed her parents lots of money, a debt that Bob now shared. These matters would have weighed heavily on her. Left unresolved, her guilt threatened their future together.

In addition to these actions, which had fractured her moral compass, Ruth had done other things, not as ethically problematic but nevertheless hurtful. At the last minute and without explanation she had canceled a highly anticipated visit to Bob. She hardly wrote when he was at sea. She confused his rank. She ignored his numerous questions. She didn't bother to comment on his feverish search for housing.

Whether the fallout from Ruth's persistent passivity was intentional or not, it had left Bob demoralized. Since he had considered all his own plans—for sea duty, officer training, flight school—as contingent upon hers, her many silences about her plans had kept him from making decisions about his future. Putting his life on hold as he waited for her had done nothing but feed his frustration. Of course, he could have gone ahead on his own. But this would have, he felt, jeopardized his future with Ruth. And he was obsessed with her. Twice when he had tried to end the relationship, he was miserable. So he kept on waiting.

Bob had other issues to deal with. Did he really forgive Ruth for her indiscretions, as he claimed, or would his resentment smolder?

Even if he had forgiven her, could he rebuild his trust in her? And what about his decisions to pass up opportunities for training or advancement while waiting for her to join him? Would he blame her for his having kept his life on hold for so many years?

Other issues they shared: Would they be able to trust each other to keep the marital vows they had exchanged? Bob was all too familiar with the escapades of married folk that "make me sick." How could he know whether he and Ruth would be different? With the two now together, they couldn't resort to using geographic distance as a an excuse not to deal with their mutual fidelity.

The initial euphoria of being together would have distracted them from these deeper issues for only so long. As euphoria gave way to the everyday, then what? Would they pull these skeletons from the closet and deal with them or would they leave the closet door closed?

"You'd Go Nuts"

Then there were the hard realities of daily life. Bob's office hours undoubtedly continued to be as grinding as ever. He regularly had to work late into the evening, day after punishing day; her arrival wouldn't have changed that. As for Ruth, although she had written months previously that she looked forward to developing her cooking skills and setting up the household, those activities alone would be unlikely to occupy all her waking hours. Bob had been consistently supportive of her working outside the home. If she did, what could she do?

Nurses were scarce to the point of crisis. By 1944 a shortage of one hundred thousand nurses nationwide had become so acute that, in his January 1945 State of the Union address, Franklin Roosevelt proposed amending the Selective Service Act to draft nurses. The public agreed—a Gallup poll revealed a whopping 73 percent approved a draft for nurses.

San Francisco likely participated in the shortage, and Ruth could probably have had her choice of jobs if she had qualified. But without her nursing degree, that was impossible. As for positions like nurse's aide, in the 1940s these jobs were not just difficult but were perceived as particularly menial. Even so, many of the positions were filled by volunteers who worked other jobs and felt it their duty to help.[9] The Ruth of these letters wouldn't have been tempted.

Teaching was the other major option of the time for educated women, but what was Ruth qualified to teach? Other possibilities would have included jobs that World War II had opened up to women for the first time, such as secretarial and clerical work. But "jobs, like housing, were extremely scarce for military wives, for no employer wanted to hire someone whose reason for being there might soon be gone."[10] Ruth lacked secretarial training, so it is unlikely that she would have considered this line of work. Besides, Bob's secretarial skills had become finely honed. Would she have wanted to have a job so similar to his? Factory work was another area that the war had recently opened to women. But, again, Ruth would likely have felt factory work to be beneath her. Housecleaning carried lower status yet. Restaurant service might have been another possibility, but "'girls holding these jobs are viewed askance by the respectable.'"[11] And, with Bob's knowledge of Bay Area bars, he would certainly have vetoed the slightest notion that she work in one of those.

Then there was the reality of wartime. San Francisco, like the other California port cities, was packed to the gills and beyond with many thousands of military wives. The lucky ones, like Ruth, found places to stay; others were driven to tenement-like extremities or worse. In those overcrowded conditions a finicky job seeker might well be overwhelmed by the competition.

So Ruth likely found herself stuck. She had just enough education and experience to make many positions unappealing but not enough to match the kind of job she considered appropriate. What Bob had written months previously may have been prophetic. With nothing to do all day long, she just might "go nuts."

"I Might as Well Answer All Such Questions Regardless of My Constitutional Rights"

However long their initial euphoria lasted, it suffered a blow within a few short weeks when Ruth received a letter from her lawyer in Minneapolis. The judge in *Schmidt v. Equitable Life Assurance* had ruled, and Ruth was indeed required to answer those distressing questions. She had been ordered to appear on November 6 in Milwaukee for continuation of the deposition.

The lawyers on both sides had mercifully come up with a plan to keep Ruth from having to return east. They sent her a set of questions and proposed answers "based on information which we have in our files and which we are sure is accurate." They asked her to sign these answers under oath and to return them for use in the case if it went to trial. If she did so, "then we will agree that no further steps will be taken by us to compel her to return to Wisconsin or Minnesota or elsewhere, in connection with this case, and we further agree that if for any reason the case is not tried, we will return the signed questions and answers to her and not file them with the Court."

Ruth kept this letter and a copy of her response, but the box includes no such signed questions and answers. Either they were not returned to her, or they were returned and she destroyed them.

The typewritten copy of her response bears the notation "RL:crl" at the bottom—a convention indicating that "RL" (Ruth Larson) was the author and "crl" (Carl Robert Larson) was the secretary. The text of her response letter, however, reflects the imprint of

Bob's years of experience in typing letters related to court-martial proceedings. Bob likely wrote it with input from Ruth.

The letter states that Ruth would sign the answers sent by the lawyers. But she continued to feel that "I am being forced to give answers which are degrading," and so she wondered, again, "if I have a constitutional right to refuse to answer such questions." Further, she wondered if the questions were "the ones which the court has ordered that I should answer" and, further still, "in my mind it is questionable whether or not they tend to prove anything in the case at issue." In short, she would sign but under protest.

"On the other hand," the letter continued, "I appreciate that as a practical matter there might be good reason to answer such questions." One reason was her friend Veronica, who "might be called to testify, and she might do greater injustice to me than the actual facts call for." Thus, she concluded, "If the facts with reference to my pregnancy can be developed by other witnesses, and if they would thereby tend to harm me more than if my own version is also included, then I might as well answer all such questions regardless of my constitutional rights, if any."

Yet agreeing to sign off on the answers wouldn't have settled everything. As the letter goes on to explain, even though "Doctor [Schmidt] and [Veronica], in attending the abortion, acted illegally, and, that, although my submission thereto might not be a violation of law (which I do not know definitely)," Ruth could foresee that "such a fact might be the basis of my being turned down for a degree as a registered nurse." So, with great reluctance, she signed and then asked her lawyer to consider not submitting the answers anyway, leaving the matter to his "good judgment."[12]

I wonder about the impact that writing this letter had on Bob and Ruth, forcing them to relive a profoundly traumatic and threatening time in their relationship. I wonder, too, how they navigated the thorny terrain of starting their marriage face to face; how Ruth passed her time; how the two of them got along.

On October 26, 1944, Bob extended his enlistment in the Coast Guard for another two years. As the war in the Pacific stormed into its bloodiest stages—Burma, Leyte, Okinawa—the work in San Francisco must have become even more frenetic.

"Discharge from the U.S. Coast Guard Is Recommended"

In May 1945 Germany surrendered and in August Japan surrendered, ending World War II. The dead have been estimated at fifteen million military personnel and thirty-five million civilians. Those who survived wanted nothing more than to hurry home and try to erase their memories of the carnage. Now the San Francisco office was busier than ever, this time processing millions of returning troops. How did stateside servicemen feel when they saw the haunted eyes and the wounds that wouldn't heal?

What Bob saw made him sick. His service records show that on October 1 he was admitted to the hospital for "abdominal pain, gas, sour regurgitation and marked nervousness." These symptoms intensified a recurring problem. In several letters over the years he had mentioned his need for antacids, and he reported numerous instances of "not knowing what to do with myself," having a "case of the nerves," or being nervous. This time he was hospitalized for eight days. The hospital discharge report included the diagnosis "anxiety state, mild." The symptoms had started one year previously, the report said, but they "always disappear when [Bob] is off duty and relaxed" so he was deemed fit for duty. Since Bob's anxiety was work related, the doctor recommended that he be reassigned.

Instead he went back to the same job for another week and then was granted an annual leave, his first leave since the wedding more than seventeen months earlier. But then something mysterious happened. A Board of Medical Survey report dated October 22—six days into the thirty-day leave period, when one might have thought that Bob and Ruth were off relaxing together somewhere—appears in Bob's military records. The BMS was the entity that reviewed physicians' recommendations for discharge from the service, and its report asserted that Bob had attempted to return to duty but found it impossible; the board recommended discharge. What happened to the leave? What happened to the mild anxiety, which had suddenly become (according to the BMS report) "psychoneurosis, anxiety state, severe." What was going on?

My guess is that Bob wanted out. With the war over he probably saw continuing in the Coast Guard as unappealing. He had never been gung-ho for the military anyway. With the war over, too, millions of returning servicemen would be flooding the job market. The longer he stayed in the Coast Guard, the less chance he would have of finding a job when he got out. The biggest reason, though, was his emotional condition. His insides churned and he was exhausted.

I believe that Bob wanted to get out of the service, and his recent hospitalization provided just the opportunity he needed. All that would be necessary to engineer a discharge for himself would be a little finagling. And that was something Bob had learned how to do. Since late August he had been assigned to Separation Center #12, where he processed forms for personnel being discharged from the service. He would have quickly learned what worked to get that type of request approved.

To create a serious enough condition to warrant discharge, Bob would have to ramp up the severity of the conditions reported by the hospital. Here is the relevant portion of the Board of Medical Survey report; I have used boldface to highlight the changes from the hospital version:

This Chief Yeoman entered the hospital on 1 October, 1945, complaining of nervousness and of epigastric pain. He dates the onset of his symptoms to **fourteen or fifteen months** ago when he began to notice epigastric pain, sour regurgitation and abdominal discomfort which occurred whenever he was under nervous tension. This condition was relieved by rest and by anti-acids. His past history reveals that **he has always been a nervous individual and had enuresis to the age of eight, was a nail-biter until the age of eleven**. In spite of his nervousness, he was able to adjust normally. At the present time he is **intensely** nervous, restless, **emotionally unstable, and breaks down into tears when under tension. He is unable to sleep and when he does fall asleep, he is disturbed by nightmares.**

He was discharged from the hospital on 9 October, 1945 and **attempted to return to duty. However, all his symptom have become markedly exaggerated and he finds it absolutely impossible to remain on duty.**

Because of his **severe** anxiety state, he would **remain unfit for military duty,** therefore **discharge from the U.S Coast Guard is recommended.**

Stylistic factors add to my belief that Bob had a hand in this document. The hospital report describes Bob as having "marked nervousness." This description becomes generalized and intensified in the BMS report: "All of his symptoms have become markedly exaggerated." The adjective becomes an adverb applied indiscriminately to "all of his symptoms." And the word *exaggerated* could well have been a stab at the term *exacerbated*. Similarly the adverb *absolutely* seems oddly unmedical when attached to "impossible to remain on duty." The intensifiers seem to reflect more the style of a chief yeoman than that of a medical doctor.

Two other bits of anecdotal evidence illustrate Bob's ability to beat the system. The first, a story he told me several times (and that appears nowhere in Ruth's collection): A sailor seeking a promotion had to take the required shorthand test, but his shorthand was bad. So he asked Bob for help and they hatched a plan. On the day of the test the sailor sat in the exam room next to an open window. While the test was being given, Bob sat outside the window, taking down the dictation in shorthand. Then, when the proctor wasn't looking, the sailor tossed his scribbles out the window to Bob who tossed in his shorthand. "And you know what?" he always concluded while looking me in the eye. "They never found out."

The second bit of evidence comes from the 1970s television comedy M*A*S*H. Whenever the company clerk Radar O'Reilly jiggered papers to work the system, Dad would chuckle, turn to me, and declare: "That's how it was. We did that too." He was proud of having beaten the system.

And I was proud to see him this way. Proud? How can I be so hypocritical? How can I be so upset with Ruth's unethical behavior while I laud Bob for his? He had provided the muscle for his fellow Coastie to cheat. Why wasn't I as upset about that? After all, under other circumstances I am just as bothered by cheating as by lying. I think family lore is at work once more. For decades I absorbed the notion that that's the way Dad was. My father modeled this behavior, and I was as comfortable with it as children generally are comfortable with whatever their family's prevailing ethos might be.

Now, in fairness, I have to come clean. If Ruth's lying troubled me, Bob's cheating must too. Particularly if, say, a grandchild were to ask for my opinion about what Bob did, I would have to say he was wrong. Still, I can't help but admire him for pulling it off and not getting caught. My mixed feelings reflect my own flawed ethics.

I don't know if Bob was proud of my ethics, but I know he was proud of my education. The mechanic's helper without a degree passed up many opportunities during the war. From electrician's training to flight training to officer training, he considered and rejected numerous ways of getting ahead, usually in the hope that, if he stayed put, Ruth would appear. Still, Ruth's ambitions for Bob—and, perhaps, his own for himself—had lasting impact.

From the letters I now understand how he transformed himself from high school near-dropout to the father who always steadfastly supported every interest of his children in education. His time in the Coast Guard had given him firsthand experience with how education could shape lives. This understanding on the part of my father had, unbeknown to me, shaped my own life as his son.

I remember once announcing to my father that I wanted to follow him and work in the elevator business after I graduated from high school. He retorted that my plan wasn't a good idea, not at all, and that I had better rid myself of it immediately. He went on to explain that I would get much further in life if I got an education, and he put his money behind those words. I received the clear message that my father wanted me to have the education that he never had.

Whatever the provenance of Bob's discharge papers, they worked. On December 4, 1945, the U.S. Coast Guard granted Chief Yeoman Carl Robert Larson an "honorable discharge, physical disability."

"He Was Never the Same After That"

This new information—the first time I had learned anything about my father's discharge from the Coast Guard—took me back to a summer day in the 1980s. My mother and I were relaxing on the dock at the family cottage in Upper Michigan when she volunteered a story. After she had joined Bob in San Francisco, she soon discovered that the happy-go-lucky guy she had known was a different man. He had become snippy and sarcastic, and she found him more difficult to be around. When I asked her what had happened, she struggled for words. I remember the phrase "nervous breakdown" because it struck me with such force. I also remember her saying, "He was never the same after that."

I was astounded. I had never heard the story before, and I would never hear it again. I couldn't understand why such an important story hadn't been part of family lore.

I also found it hard to believe. By the time I reached adulthood, I had grown accustomed to knowing my father as emotionally dead. Though rationally I knew better, I struggled to perceive him as having feelings, let alone nerves. And if that was the case, how could they "break down"? Also, the phrase "nervous breakdown" frustrated me. What did that 1940s-era phrase connote? An anxiety disorder? Depression? Burnout? A combination of these? Something else? Though I am separated from my father's experiences and lack expertise in psychiatric diagnosis, I suspect that he suffered from extreme fatigue from working long hours, from anxiety about his future, and from depression stemming from his helplessness in the face of devastating situations. Though the phrase "nervous breakdown" has become passé among doctors nowadays, it seems especially suitable to describe the complex nature of Bob's trauma.[13]

Throughout my youth and young adulthood, I was troubled by my father's difficulty expressing warmth or love—really, *any* positive emotion—toward me. I was confident enough of my place as his son to know that there was love there somewhere, but I was confused by his inability to express it, except on the rarest of occasions. The resulting hurt and frustration clouded our years together. Now that I know what happened at a profoundly vulnerable time of his life, however, I understand him better. In his passion for Ruth he opened himself in the most naked way imaginable, only to be repeatedly hurt. If my father could have shared with me his feelings of vulnerability, I might have found warmth in the connection with my own feelings of insecurity, and our relationship could have deepened.

I know this because something like this did happen. I was thirty-six and had just learned that, after five effective years in a teaching-research position, my contract wouldn't be renewed. That summer my dad and I spent several hours on the road together. He started telling me about his work situation at Otis years previously. With story after story he shared feelings of frustration with bosses, of working to gain their trust, of his seemingly ever-present fear of being fired. None of this had been part of family lore, but he responded to my need for support in my time of professional vulnerability. So he introduced me to new stories—new to me, anyway—that spoke to me deeply. Growing in my understanding of his difficulties helped me to get through mine, and our relationship matured.

With the new information about Bob's discharge, I now had a context to better understand my mother's story on the dock and my emotionally distant father. I had always assumed that his ethnic heritage was responsible for his detachment, trading on the stereotype of the dour Swede. Also, by the time I was old enough to have had experiences of him significant enough to remember, he was entering middle age and beyond. I figured that the years had encrusted him with reserve.

Still, the news of a nervous breakdown drove me to rethink matters. Something definitely happened to or, more precisely, *in* my father during the war. But family lore told me, and his service records confirmed, that he hadn't seen combat. So what could have caused the trauma?

As early as September 1942, before he had been in the war for a year, he declared that "this place is getting on my nerves." This comment proved to be far more than a glib expression of a fleeting annoyance. Rather, the nerves problem returned again and again. At one point Bob recounted this story: "I've been feeling pretty blue all week so yesterday while I was laying on my bunk just resting one of our boys, Eddie, came over and wanted to know what was wrong. I told him nothing but he says for me to come in the recreation room with him and he'll play the piano for me to relax my mind. Gee, it was really wonderful."

Eddie played for two hours; Bob's need must have been both extreme and visible.

Less than two months later Bob's situation had reached the point that "I'm so nervous now my stomach's starting to play tricks on me." He continued to take antacids, probably off and on, until his last hospitalization for anxiety in October 1945, before his discharge from the service. I don't believe that an anxious temperament alone caused the problem. It took a war.

I believe that the nervous breakdown Bob experienced included combat—not visible combat in the Pacific but invisible combat in his heart. A World War II veteran of an infantry medical detachment wrote to me: "As a soldier not facing death I felt constant guilt at being safe while processing death tags." Bob didn't process death tags; perhaps worse, he processed papers that sent men to their deaths. For nearly four years he had spent long hours sending thousands of young men away to fight, yet he was powerless to prevent even one from dying. This invisible combat left its mark. It was a source of the wound that my mother described to me and of the scar that I later experienced as my father's emotional distance. Like a piece of shrapnel never removed, that invisible wound blocked access to his feelings.

The letters point to another source of Bob's emotional trauma. During those same long years, he endured an onslaught in another way—passive resistance from the woman he loved. "If you only knew," he wrote in May 1942 when Ruth had canceled a visit with a vague excuse at the last minute. The phrase identified an attitude that he would see repeated again and again: Ruth's pursuing relationships with other men, ignoring his questions, confusing his rank, and postponing important decisions. She claimed to love him but treated him as if she didn't.

Then there was the pregnancy. It confirmed Bob's worst fears and posed the greatest challenge to Ruth and Bob's relationship. I can't imagine the pain of that emotional terrain. The only thing that kept them together, I believe, was his obsessive belief that he couldn't live without her. He wrote that he forgave her, but could he forget? The suspicion expressed in his later letters suggests that he couldn't.

Ruth's prolonged difficulties in reaching important decisions could only have complicated matters. Bob wasn't indecisive about marriage; he was eager to marry her. She apparently wasn't ready to marry him or anyone else; nor, however, was she ready to let him go.

Ruth apparently also did not understand the impact of her indecision and lack of forthrightness on Bob. While he waited for her to decide, he put his own life on hold. Eventually he was able to express some of that frustration when in March 1944 he wrote, "If I'd ever dreamed you'd never have come out before now I'd never have come ashore." With her myriad delays came the end of many possibilities for advancement, all sacrificed to her difficulty in making up her mind and her inability to be candid with him.

Bob put his life on hold for the sake of his hopes while Ruth responded with passivity, evasion, and betrayal. And, though she wrote that she loved him, her love was "a little different" and "maybe not the way you love me." Such contrasting ways of interacting— Bob completely and utterly committed, Ruth indecisive and evasive—played cruel tricks on him. His unrequited love had nowhere to go but frustration, then to anger and alienation. To shield himself against these feelings, he shut down emotionally. Thus I believe that the way she treated him contributed to his trauma.

At the same time Bob can't be relieved of the role that he played. Despite years of frustration and disappointment, he remained in the relationship. Not only that, he practiced his own brand of passivity by keeping his life on hold for years while awaiting Ruth's plans. Perpetually postponing his future limited his options and, I believe, intensified his sense of desperation.

Then, after Ruth joined Bob in the fall of 1944, his vulnerability likely increased because he no longer could take refuge in a goddess-like vision of an idolized sweetheart. His oft-repeated refrain, that dreaming of her kept him from "going nuts," may have been more than sentimentalism. It may have been a strategy to cope with a situation that he would otherwise have found unbearable. But with Ruth's all-too-human presence, the strategy no longer worked.

All these factors, I believe, set the stage for an emotional breakdown. Bob probably succumbed to a type of posttraumatic stress disorder.

Ruth's brother Ebert—whom both Bob and Ron had hoped to meet during the war—suffered an even more debilitating wound. Although Ebert served in Europe, like Bob he didn't experience combat. Still, the war blew him apart. While searching family papers to supplement Ruth's letters, I learned that Ebert was honorably discharged in 1945, lived unstably for a year, then reenlisted. After he had gone AWOL for a second time and faced a court-martial, Werner wrote to Ebert's commanding officer on August 1, 1947:

> Our son, so bright, so promising, so hopeful, so jolly, so well liked, and always so faithful to duty, now wanders away from

duty, not knowing what he is doing, constantly thinking and brooding yet arriving at no conclusion, bewildered and wandering in his mind. He never was the same boy after he came back from Europe. Five (almost) years of world war two seems to have ruined him. I cannot finish this letter for tears. Emotions get the best of me.

Surely you won't punish him for losing his mind in the service of his country. Some gave their life, some their limbs while others will walk the rest of their life in perpetual darkness. Will our son ever again regather his bewildered mental powers?

He didn't. I know this because Uncle Ebert lived with us, off and on, in my childhood. During summers in Upper Michigan he would take me fishing, teaching me the nuances of bobber, sinker, and cane pole. I remember longing for the day when I could match his skill in catching a stringer of panfish. Much of the time, though, Uncle Ebert stared out the window. I wondered what he thought about for such long spans.

Uncle Ebert used to play a game with me I didn't like. He called out, "Bruce?" When I answered, he responded an octave lower in his gravelly bass, "Da goooose." Then he laughed and I squirmed. He seemed pleased to make a joke at my expense, a stunt he repeated whenever he could catch me off guard.

It wasn't until I was working on this book that I realized Uncle Ebert's way of belittling me mirrored my father's response to my drooping pants when I was a toddler. The sample is far too small for any conclusions; yet I still must ask: Did the troubled outcomes from their wartime experiences suggest the same proclivity to humiliate? Playing on my vulnerability as a boy, they got me to experience for a brief moment the powerlessness that they experienced for years during the war. Involving me in their humiliation may have provided them with a feeling of momentary redemption.

They had initiated me into a fellowship of humiliation, demeaning me to make meaning for themselves.

Today the U. S. Department of Veteran Affairs offers benefits for noncombatants diagnosed with PTSD. However, during World War II the condition now known as PTSD was called battle fatigue. Since Bob hadn't seen combat, "battle fatigue" couldn't describe his condition—thus the hospital report's diagnosis of job-related anxiety. This insufficient diagnosis kept him, and thousands of other noncombatants with similar symptoms, from being recognized as a casualty of war. It also prevented him from receiving treatment. I believe that the disorder remained.

Updating Family Lore

I didn't have to linger long over the question of why such a significant experience as my father's nervous breakdown had been left out of family lore. Like most parents, mine wanted me to view them as exemplars. Sharing memories that expose their vulnerability doesn't do that. Or so the typical reasoning goes.

In my experience the opposite is true. When my mother told me on the dock about Bob's nervous breakdown, and when my father shared his job experiences during that long conversation in the car, their expressions of vulnerability drew me closer. Not only that, they educated me. Learning that my parents experienced difficulties yet survived inspired me to do likewise. If they had remained content portraying everything as all sweetness and light, when I encountered sourness and dark, family lore would have been of no use. But when my parents shared those experiences that affirmed vulnerability and finitude, I stood a better chance of coping. Even more, I felt loved.

I don't mean to imply that my parents should have shared with me every vulnerable experience from their past. They needed to maintain boundaries that protected their privacy, and not all their past experiences spoke to a specific situation. The little that they did share, though, was golden.

I now understand why my parents couldn't update family lore very far. I believe the anxiety and anger, the guilt and shame from the war years remained unresolved. The effect of those feelings remained with them and influenced their relationship. Though I had long wished to learn more about their lives during the war years, I now know why I didn't. The pain that they remembered was too great, the risk of sharing it too high.

The opportunity to read and absorb these letters has filled in much of the gap. Now I can understand Bob, that young man who was able to express such a gamut of emotions—from love, happiness, playfulness, tenderness, and exultation to fear, anger, suspicion, loneliness, and despair. I was both surprised and fascinated to find him this way, contradicting most of my personal experience of him when he was older.

Now, too, I can view my father's honorable discharge as one link in the chain of stress and exhaustion that bound him during the war. He may have had to contend with anxiety from his childhood—the bed-wetting and nail biting mentioned in the BMS report suggest this. But when the anxiety threatened to become overwhelming, as it seemed to have during the war, he indeed became overwhelmed. He had to slam the door on his feelings in order to survive.

That is why, I believe, he appeared so emotionally flat in later life. When there arose what I now see, in retrospect, as times of difficulty, he never mentioned anxiety nor did I observe him exhibiting it. All he spoke of was exhaustion, often before falling asleep on the couch. Did his wartime experiences teach him to muffle anxiety with fatigue? I think so. Those experiences created the paradigm that he probably used for the rest of his life.

The vulnerable part of Bob's history, so different from the lore of my family, was affirmed by an unexpected source, a dream I had as I neared the completion of this book. In the dream I approached an apartment where he and my mother lived, a place unfamiliar to me. As I entered and announced my arrival, he poked his head around the corner from the next room, stood up, and walked out to greet me. I saw in his eyes a deep tenderness that I had never seen before. I sensed that he knew I had read the letters. He seemed pleased to be free of their secrets, pleased that I now knew what had been kept hidden for so long. We hugged and then I awoke, in tears.

•

After Bob's discharge from the Coast Guard, he returned to the Otis Elevator Company and the couple settled in Chicago. No longer a mechanic's helper, he put the savvy and drive that had blossomed in the service to good use as a salesman. In the highly competitive downtown market, which was poised to experience a boom in new construction, a knowledgeable and persistent salesman could land plenty of new contracts. Bob did so well that in several years he was promoted to sales manager of the Chicago office.

As Bob's career grew, so did the family—my sister was born in 1946, with my brother and me following in 1949 and 1953, respectively. We moved to Lombard, a village twenty miles west of the Loop. Bob commuted by train while Ruth took care of the children and managed the household. After Werner's death in 1955, Lilly came to live with us.

Meanwhile Bob surveyed his future with Otis and didn't like what he saw. Every man above him on the promotion ladder was overweight, drinking heavily, or had suffered a heart attack. Bob's hospitalization for an ulcer when I was in elementary school provided the necessary wake-up call. Bob and a partner left Otis and bought Goetz Elevator, a small company in decline. The move entailed great risk since Bob wouldn't draw a salary until the company turned a big enough profit. For the family to get by, Ruth would have to find a paying job, her first since her stint at Two Rivers. Having finally earned her nursing degree, she found work at a nearby high school. After two or three years the business became profitable, but Ruth kept working. She enjoyed her job.

These were prime years for Ruth and Bob. They had made it through the lean times, and then we children left the nest, one by one, for college. Bob realized his dream of flying: he took lessons, earned his pilot's license, and bought an airplane. Ruth drew confidence from her nursing work. Eventually Bob sold the business, and the couple moved into a long and productive retirement. The nonprofit flying service that they started, Northwoods AirLifeline, grew to provide critical medical transportation for hundreds of people across the Upper Peninsula. The sixty-one-year marriage ended only with Bob's death in 2006.

By external indicators Bob and Ruth had succeeded. I can't answer, or even begin to evaluate, whether their marriage was satisfying. The marriage was theirs; they are the only ones who could say. Yet from all that I have learned in writing this book, I can't imagine that their relationship developed very far. Those first months of marriage started out with the same dysfunctional patterns that had persisted throughout their engagement. Perhaps the couple navigated the numerous sensitive areas by avoidance in order to simply go on. But perseverance by itself is no virtue, especially given the pervasiveness and depth of their problems. Perhaps they at least were able to persevere about persevering, inspiring themselves by how they could keep going together against the odds.

But I don't think they ever broke free from the damage they experienced in their young adult years. This damage, repressed and unexamined, kept them from fully engaging in relationships that meant most to them. I observed many times, for example, my father's speaking more kindly to a waitress than he did to his wife. At the time I was baffled; now I surmise that, since a waitress couldn't hurt him, he could risk showing her kindness. In contrast, Ruth had hurt him—deeply, profoundly—and could do so again. So he kept his distance.

I also better understand my father's emotional distance toward me. Now, I realize, had it not been for what happened to him during those war years, he could well have lived with the lively openness I encountered in the letters. Now I have grounds for imagining him that way and grounds for an explanation of what happened. This brings me a sense of resolution.

Much less so with Ruth. While I first thought her behavior represented a postponed adolescent rebellion, I haven't been able to hold on to that conclusion. Now I can't imagine that, once married, she stopped lying, denying, or deceiving. In fact almost everything in the letters suggests the opposite. Marriage did little to change her relationship with Bob, so why would I think that it changed anything else? If it did not change anything, then I am stumped by how well she hid from me her deceptive habit. How did she do it?

I think it was Ruth's passivity, again, that proved to be so effective. The summer after the wedding, for example, when she needed to decide how she would finish her nursing program and when to join her husband, she pulled back and coasted—ambling through her job, working on her suntan, wondering about her marriage. When she finally realized that she needed to decide something, still in passive mode, she asked Bob to decide for her. When he did, she ignored him—passive again. Passivity got her through that time, and I believe it continued to get her through in her relationship with Bob and later with me. This may explain why I never detected that she deceived me or ever witnessed her deceiving anyone else. Passive under my radar, she didn't need to.

Messing with family lore is not for the timid. It required that I change how I understood my parents fundamentally. Sometimes this brought excitement, as when I learned of my father's expressing a range of emotions, engaging life with such verve while overcoming huge obstacles to achieve his heart's desire. This richness echoed within me reassuringly, inspiring me. At other times it brought distress. I didn't want to know, for example, that my mother betrayed my father. And I didn't want to admit that she engaged in a pattern of deception.

The longer the journey over this unexpected terrain continued, the more I came to realize that I couldn't return to the parents I had known. They had evolved into more complex people. But this came at a price. I can no longer lean back into a version of family lore that's neat and tidy, full of "just so" tales. Loose ends still dangle. Questions remain unanswered. No happy ending appears. Indeed there is no ending.

Acknowledgments

I am profoundly grateful to Clyde Henry—whose thoughtful conversations on the manuscript encouraged me and whose website savvy saved me from digital despair—and to others who took the time to read and comment on parts or all of the manuscript: John Barber, Ed Beers, Steve Boggs, John Colvin, Lilian Cooper, Dennis Hatfield, Brenda Holbrook, Carol Hunter, John Larson, Mac Marshall, the Ohio Writers Guild, Nancy Woodson, and Christian Zacher. I profited from their comments and support; I alone am responsible for the result.

When I needed to recover some obscured portions of Ruth's letters, Julia Barber recommended the document restorers at the Intermuseum Conservation Association in Cleveland, who made valuable suggestions. Peg Barber, with her command of photographic software, made the passages appear crystal clear.

I am thankful to others who lent their support in a variety of ways: Emily Beers, Dave Biesel, Russ Bryan, Jim Burklo, Jerry Cooper, Sandy Crooms, Karen Donato, Neil Donato, Ruth Evenson, Janet Henry, Laura Jenks, Sarah Jenks, Mary Lou Nelson, Tony Robinson, Mary Russell, Bob Shadel, Sylvia Shadel, and all those who asked, "How's your book coming?" Special thanks to the Columbus Arts Festival for the opportunity to read from this book on the Word Is Art stage, to Shan Thompson for generously contributing his expertise and advice to the book's website, and to the men in the Columbus Men's Group for their supportive brotherhood.

Acknowledgments

The Minnesota Historical Society sent microfilm of Minneapolis newspapers from the 1940s to the Columbus Public Library, which gave me access to them. The Lester Public Library, Two Rivers, made available contemporaneous articles from the local newspaper. The National Personnel Records Center, National Archives and Records Administration, St. Louis, supplied Bob's service records. The Office of the Registrar, University of Minnesota, sent Ruth's transcript. Federal and state courts in Minnesota and Wisconsin scoured their records for the [Schmidt] v. Equitable Life Assurance Company lawsuit.

My heartfelt thanks to Gary Kass, acquisitions editor for the University of Missouri Press. He and his readers led me graciously and patiently through revisions of the manuscript with the utmost professionalism. Thanks also to copy editor Polly Kummel. She made many helpful suggestions and improved the readability of the manuscript. Sara Davis, Lyn Smith, Greg Haefner, and Stephanie Williams performed wonders in producing the book in final form.

I thank Bob and Ruth Larson, my parents, for raising me and loving me. I consider what I have written a gesture of thanksgiving to them for what I have learned.

Finally I thank my beloved spouse, Katherine Larson. For the hundreds of hours we discussed the letters, for her help with research and editorial acumen, for her emotional support and inspiration, I am filled with the deepest gratitude.

Questions for Discussion

1. How did World War II affect the options and choices available to Ruth and Bob?
2. Why do you think that Ruth dated so much during her engagement?
3. Why do you think Bob continued in the relationship after learning of Ruth's many dates and pregnancy? Would you have done the same thing? Why or why not?
4. How did the long periods of separation affect Ruth and Bob individually? As a couple?
5. How would you have responded to Werner as your father? To Lilly as your mother? If you had been Ruth's parent, how would you have reacted as the story unfolded?
6. Stan wrote that the John Schmidt tragedy should be remembered "for the lesson that it teaches." What do you think that lesson might be?
7. If Bob and Ruth had not married on May 3, 1944, imagine what might have happened.
8. How do you think this story would have played out if today's electronic media had been available then?
9. The author doubts that Bob and Ruth's marriage was a good idea. What do you think?
10. The author finds it ironic from a twenty-first-century perspective that Ruth may have sought to achieve freedom through marriage. What does he mean? Do you agree?

11. Were you surprised when Werner accompanied Ruth to the deposition in Milwaukee? Why or why not?

12. How did being a "mama's boy" affect the author's response to what he learned about his mother in the letters?

13. Do you agree with the author's decision to make "the whole truth" known about his parents, or should he have left some of it out of the book? If the latter, what should he have left out? Why?

14. What do you imagine will happen to personal mementos (letters, photos, diaries, journals) that you may leave after your death? Is this what you want, or would you prefer that something else be done? If so, what?

Notes

At the End, in the Beginning

1. Adam Kirsch, "The Battle for History," *New York Times Book Review*, May 29, 2011, 11.

Then, Now

1. Norma Ellen Knox Anderson, "1942 Norma Ellen Knox (Anderson)," http://www.nursing.umn.edu/alumni/nursing-memories/1942-norma-ellen-knox-anderson/index.htm; Ellen Wolfson, "1944 Memory from Ellen Wolfson, RN," http://www.nursing.umn.edu/alumni/nursing-memories/1944-memory-from-ellen-wolfson/index.htm; Betty Howson Heinemann, "Class of 1945 Memories from Virginia Heinzmann," http://www.nursing.umn.edu/alumni/nursing-memories/class-of-1945-memories-from-virginia-heinzmann/index.htm; Shirley Small, "1945 Memory from Shirley Small," http://www.nursing.umn.edu/alumni/nursing-memories/1945MemoryfromShirleySmall/index.htm; Verle Waters Clark, "Class of 1948 Memories as Shared by Verle (Hambleton) Waters Clark," http://www.nursing.umn.edu/alumni/nursing-memories/Classof1948/index.htm, all in Alumni Nursing Memories section of University of Minnesota School of Nursing website.

2. Richard Miller, "The Story of Treasure Island (Part 2)," *Treasure Island Music Festival*, 2011, http://www.treasureislandfestival.com/2011/the-island-pt-2/.

Notes

3. Ibid.

4. Jerry Siegel and Joe Shuster, "Just Like a Woman," *Superman*, May 21, 1941.

5. David M. Kennedy, *Freedom from Fear: The American People in Depression and War, 1929–1945* (New York: Oxford University Press, 1999), 781.

6. Richard R. Lingeman, *Don't You Know There's a War On?* (New York: G. P. Putnam's Sons, 1970), 90.

7. Frederick J. Taussig, *Abortion, Spontaneous and Induced: Medical and Social Aspects* (St. Louis: C. V. Mosby, 1936), 26.

8. See Leslie J. Reagan, *When Abortion Was a Crime: Women, Medicine, and Law in the United States, 1867–1973* (Berkeley: University of California Press, 1997), 160–73.

9. Doris Weatherford, *American Women and World War II* (New York: Facts on File, 1990), 18–20.

10. Ibid., 271.

11. Ibid., 272; Weatherford is quoting Gretta Palmer, "Marriage and Work," *Ladies Home Journal*, March 1942, 111.

12. Although I contacted every court in which this case could have been filed, I never was able to find records revealing the outcome. Either it was settled or the records were destroyed.

13. For an excellent review of the concept, see Megan Barke, Rebecca Fribush, and Peter N. Stearns, "Nervous Breakdown in Twentieth-Century American Culture," *Journal of Social History* 33, no. 3 (2000): 565–84.